MERGING SPIRITUALITY WITH QUANTUM CONSCIOUSNESS

Manifest Your Life Consciously

Bente Hansen

BALBOA.PRESS

A DIVISION OF HAY HOUSE

Special Thanks

Thank you Michael James Heath for the amazing vibrant painting, *Love From A Light Being,* that you gifted for the cover of this book. You are that special person who came into my life when I needed a friend, a friend who accepts my quirkiness and other-worldliness with equanimity and calmness. Thank you for the kindness, wisdom and patience you continually exhibit.

I am blessed to have the enduring support of friends that have been part of my journey for many years. At times I've felt uncertain, lost and definitely bewildered by the challenges of life. You've been there – solid, reliable, supportive and loving – always cajoling and encouraging me to believe in my dreams and abilities. You know who you are! However, special thanks to my soul sisters Wendy Post, Elizabeth Bailey and Janette Palladino. You've known me through thick and thin, and witnessed both the best and the worst!

Author's Note

Despite doing my best to understand and explain the power of the quantum sciences and how they relate to the concept of spirituality I know that at times I've used inaccurate language, erroneous descriptions or interpreted the functioning of scientific phenomena incorrectly. My descriptions provide a rough sketch and certainly lack finesse, and even accuracy. This means that my simplification of conceptually complex scientific phenomena may lead the reader into a state of misunderstanding, though hopefully not too much.

My narrative does not fully reflect the beauty and magic of the quantum cosmos and its true potential. It's never been my intention to mislead or misdirect the reader. If I have I apologize to the science experts in the field for the misperceptions that may arise. It's never been my intention to distort a field of study that I find fascinating, and which I have attempted to understand to the best of my ability. Hopefully the intent of my analysis and sharing holds some cohesion and relevance in shifting the perceptions held by many worldwide.

I don't see spirituality and the phenomena of mysticism as separate and distinct from the world of the quantum sciences. In fact, I believe that the field of quantum science has the potential to explain more of our origins, our true reality and ability – definitely more than any man made dogma or belief systems. Once humanity is ready to embrace the real potential that exists within then there's the possibility of expanded consciousness and functioning at higher states of awareness. This in turn has the capacity to create massive changes globally on every level.

— The day science begins to study non-physical phenomena it will make more progress in one decade than all the previous centuries of its existence —
Nikola Tesla

Introduction

The Butterfly

I had been in Kathmandu, Nepal, just a few days and my search had led me to a particular Buddhist monastery. There was no denying this was not a regular vacation jaunt. Prior to leaving Australia the messages had been flowing almost continuously from my non-physical friends. The messages were straight forward. I needed to travel to Nepal and India and basically would be required to travel to specific places where certain people would be met and incidents would occur. The specifics were extremely limited and vague. In fact, I was completely clueless and was not hopeful of achieving any particular outcomes, though was trusting that all would progress positively for the three weeks of my travels. The urging to take this trip had been overwhelmingly strong for a few months, and could not be denied. I didn't understand the inner urge, only that there was some as yet unclear reason for embarking upon a visit to these two particular countries. Consciously I had never had a yearning to travel to either Nepal or India so obviously there must have been a deeper reason for the travel.

A little while before leaving Australia unusual training had been undertaken over a period of several weeks. My non-physical friends would urge me to go for a drive. My response was to hop into the car with no preconceived idea of destination and as I drove along I would hear phrases such as "Turn right", "Turn left", "Continue", "Turn around". I was guided into suburbs and areas that I'd never previously visited and had no idea they even existed. My sense of direction was completely challenged as the commands continued to be heard in my head. There was definitely no satellite navigation, Google or hard copy street maps used in this exercise.

After driving from anywhere between thirty and sixty minutes I would eventually find myself back home. Intuitively I sensed that this was both preparation and training for what was to unfold on my trip to Nepal and India.

As the plane banked, preparing for landing, Mount Everest and the whole mountain range looked majestic and imposing as the plane neared Kathmandu. It was one of the most spectacular sights I'd ever witnessed and I took this as an omen that my travels would be fortuitous. Kathmandu was certainly chaotic, colourful and vibrant. Once settled into hotel accommodation I spent a day sightseeing and taking countless photos, all the while wondering what would happen next. Realistically there was only one way to figure out where I was to go and that was to meditate. During meditation a cryptic message came through. It would have been so much easier if the message had been delivered in simple terms, but that wasn't how it happened. The cryptic messages were my travel guide for the three week trip, with them being delivered in a timely manner on an almost daily basis. My challenge was to decipher the messages and to figure out the logistics of destination, travel, times and accommodation as the journey evolved.

In this particular instance I understood the cryptic message to mean that I was to visit a certain, as yet unidentified, monastery in the area. When there I was to seek an audience with the abbot as well as donate the children's books, crayons and stationery that I had hastily included in my luggage the day before departure. Previously I had read that basic educational materials were in limited supply in Nepal and a donation of these items would be greatly appreciated. Checking the Lonely Planet guide for Nepal was not an uplifting experience as apparently there were over a thousand monasteries in the country. There were also a large number of monasteries in and around Kathmandu, which meant my search could be likened to looking for the proverbial needle in a haystack.

Information received during a substantial number of meditation experiences was the underlying reason for my visit to an unknown monastery. Over a period of weeks I'd had several out of body experiences during daily meditation. An aspect of me, or my soul, had astral travelled to a monastery where I'd engaged in lengthy telepathic discussions with an abbot. Initially I assumed that there was some spiritual connection taking place and there was nothing more to it. The likelihood of travel to the Asian continent had not even surfaced in my awareness. However, as the out of body connections continued it became evident that my physical presence was required. Hence there was both hesitancy and excitement at finally arriving in Kathmandu. This literally was a case of "flying by the seat of my pants". There were no expectations, no aspirations. I simply felt compelled to adhere to the inner urging that had become all consuming.

The easiest way of visiting monasteries, I figured, would be to hire a local guide who surely would know the location of monasteries in the city and surrounding areas. I was in luck almost immediately in finding an English speaking guide and a day was spent driving around and exploring quite a number of possibilities. Eventually we found a monastery in the surrounding area which felt right, according to my interpretation of the cryptic clues received. My obliging guide, ever helpful, insisted on waiting while I spoke with one of the monks. The monk invited me to explore the gardens while he went inside to seek out the abbot. I was unsure that my request for an audience would be granted but nevertheless I wandered around the large gardens, admiring the profusion of colourful flowers and ornamental statues and flags that symbolize the Buddhist faith. The monastery was located on elevated land, with stunning views of Nepalese mountains nearby.

Walking along a path in the extensive gardens I came to some rough steps leading upwards and decided to explore this trail, wondering where it would lead to. As I walked slowly up the steps I mentally questioned whether this was the monastery the cryptic message had alluded to. While reflecting on this question I was also conscious of carefully watching each step as I walked upwards. The steps were narrow, roughly hewn and uneven, with vegetation and pebbles scattered everywhere so I really had no option but to look closely at each step before taking it. Suddenly, on the next step a butterfly appeared.

The butterfly hadn't flown onto the garden step. It simply appeared out of nowhere. Mouth agape I was flabbergasted. Eyes were closed and then quickly opened again. It was still there. I then closed my eyes momentarily once more and upon opening them the butterfly was gone, though there was no sign of a butterfly moving about anywhere. There was absolutely no sign of it flying away or in circles or in any direction at all. It had disappeared, in much the same way it appeared suddenly. I'd heard of materialization and de-materialization abilities but this was the first time I'd actually encountered such a phenomenon. I took it as a sign from my non-physical friends that my interpretation of the cryptic message was correct.

The whole journey throughout Nepal and India was based on interpreting cryptic messages that were delivered either in meditations, in lucid dreams or were heard in my head. What was especially magical about the trip is that from then on either a butterfly or an eagle would appear nearby, and this would be an indication of correct interpretation of the cryptic messages. These two powerful animal totems were with me constantly, and as a result the whole travel experience was a delight rather than a challenging chore.

Animals communicate messages continually and when there is something I need to know or heed I feel a shift within, as though there's added energy telling me to pay attention. Over a quarter of a century this ability to read and understand the messages and information has become clearer and sharper. But it wasn't always this way. At the very start of my awakening my sensitivity to the subtleties was practically non-existent. Like so many individuals on the planet my body was, at one time, filled with pain, uncertainty, emotional reactivity and energy heaviness. My body felt dense and my intuitive abilities were lacking the razor-like sharpness that plays such a major role in my life nowadays.

The Journey

My journey into awareness and deeper understanding was catapulted into existence by a major life change. As a very young child I astral travelled and communicated with non-physical beings, something I felt was a common experience and which I found exciting as it afforded opportunities for great adventures. Like many young children that reality was left behind once the demands of everyday Earth reality, parental expectations and the need for conformity exerted their pressure. It was not until my twenty-four year marriage ended that the voices of the non-physical companions of my early childhood once again captured my attention, and became mentors, teachers and constant companions.

Our reunion was magical and exciting. Hearing their wisdom, the gentle exhortations and guidance gave me hope for better things. I quickly realized that living what would be considered a normal life was not a perfect match for my personality. Nor did it satisfy my insatiable hunger for deeper understanding of the complexities of life, the universe and the vast unknown. The voices of the non-physical beings were heard loud and clear and so began an extraordinarily exciting and life changing journey.

Like many individuals seeking deeper meaning to life I initially read voraciously, attended workshops and undertook spiritual practices. Meditation became a regular habit, giving gratitude a daily routine; affirmations were sprouted with dedication and enthusiasm. New ways of looking at the world, learning to love myself, letting go of judgment, accepting what is, understanding and practicing detachment were all part of the process, as were countless other explorations and learning techniques.

One of the gifts I possess is an ability to clearly hear the subtle and inaudible voices outside of myself. Intuitively I knew that these were not the voices that heralded mental health issues. When I heard a voice it carried wisdom, kindness, encouragement and gentleness. Not once was there any negative suggestion given. There was never a cacophony of voices urging self-harm or creating fear. Numerous times I resisted the guidance that was gently expressed, and quickly discovered that it was not to my benefit to be dismissive or to ignore the information that was provided. This was my way of learning discernment. Basically it became a matter of testing, re-testing and validating the given information. In the early stages my conscious mind (ego) was still very much in charge, and deep seated fears were constantly running non-stop in the background of my consciousness.

Despite this, a strong desire existed to clear myself of everything that held me back from reaching my true potential and which prevented the fulfilment of attaining my life purpose. This desire was etched firmly and burned deep within. I needed to be clean, to be clear and to have no impediments to achieving whatever I had incarnated for. Of course the question was always, "What have I come here for?" or "What is my purpose?" No matter how I looked at it there were always more limitations to be cleared and more healing to be undertaken because I instinctively sensed that this process, often likened to peeling away the layers of an onion was extremely important and essential to figuring out the meaning of life.

Interestingly, the need to feel clean and clear was a driving force from deep within, one that I was unable to control or quell. Was this being fed from the conscious, sub-conscious or super-conscious levels of the mind? I truly had no idea; it was merely a compulsion that was always there. The process began simply. Physical fitness and a healthy dietary lifestyle had become important from an early age and routines were easily established and adhered to. The next phase of the clearing was obviously healing the emotional baggage, which quickly turned out to be a bottomless quagmire of deep seated fears and beliefs. The more work undertaken for healing and release the more there surfaced for further attention. This process was, and still is, an ongoing one lasting many years.

At different times in a fit of frustration with the never ending process I would rant wildly and loudly at the non-physical beings who, by this stage had become my best buddies. The weariness of dealing with the seemingly never ending truckloads of emotional baggage was overwhelming. The struggle to find deeper meaning to life entailed finding the real me, who somehow had become buried beneath mountains of grubby emotional beliefs and programming. There were moments that lasted days and even weeks as I grappled for release and further understanding. Then, suddenly and unexpectedly, it would feel as though a breakthrough in awareness occurred. Feelings of lightness and relief would flood my consciousness for a brief while. Life would once again become easier, there would be flow and things would progress smoothly.

This became a regular pattern. The ease of life, the flow, the joy would occur temporarily before once again there would be further learning, letting go and healing of deep-seated wounds. These emotional wounds would gradually percolate to the surface of my consciousness and I'd be annoyed once again with the seemingly never ending process of letting go and healing. It was in one of those moments of intense exasperation with the repeating pattern that I actually let my non-physical buddies know that I was far from impressed and I screamed, "When will it end?"

Instead of hearing words of encouragement I clairvoyantly saw a solid rock staircase in front of me. As I looked at this staircase it continued upward with absolutely no sign that there was actually an ending in sight. At that moment it was definitely not what I'd hoped to see! Feeling let down by what appeared to be a daunting journey I rapidly came to the awareness that there's no defined end to spiritual growth, expansion and understanding. Instinctively I understood that the vertical face (riser) of each step represented the struggle to evolve and the horizontal face (step) of each step represented the ease and the flow. From this it became apparent that overcoming challenges provides new opportunities for inner growth, and that this process would most likely continue on indefinitely through lifetimes. The rewards, for want of a better word, would come after the struggles. I couldn't help think that maybe there was some truth in the age old saying, "No pain, no gain".

The Layers

Peeling away the layers is a term often referred to in metaphysical and spiritual circles. A simple way of describing it is to think of a stunning gemstone. It does not start off as a precious and valuable possession. Gemstones start off as carbon, fossilized plants, various rock types and so on, and over eons of exposure to the elements, being put under pressure, exposed to heat and weather extremes somehow miraculously the beauty that's beneath the original matter and grime is transformed into a prized piece of jewellery and adornment. How it started off and how it ended is a lengthy process, involving a lot of chemical and physical processes. This change could not be possible in a short period of time, as each stage of its transformation is critical to the final outcome.

It's the same with the process of shedding the old beliefs, emotions, programming and whatever else is held within that is not authentic and pure to the soul self. These are all part of the layers of the onion analogy that is commonly mentioned in metaphysical circles. This release and fine tuning is not a journey for the faint hearted. It takes grit and determination to evolve to the stage where the extraneous baggage, on all levels, is released. When this happens there's a real shift in awareness, consciousness and understanding. This shift results in freedom, a feeling of liberation, which ultimately supports expansion, manifestation and brings greater joy to life.

Is it truly possible to become fully authentic and enlightened, with all layers completely removed and all pain and suffering released in this lifetime? According to Buddhist teachings many lifetimes of striving are needed before becoming enlightened, or reaching the state of Nirvana as it's also called. In the countless communications I've had with non-physical beings I'm beginning to see that there's another possibility. I was told that there are many traditions and beliefs that have been held and adhered to on our planet and which have offered a path to higher consciousness and enlightenment. I was told that these traditional teachings were deserving of respect. The message continued along the lines of saying that there are new and faster ways of achieving the same outcome available for use nowadays.

It would be wonderful to have a fast track method, preferably one that is both painless and joyful. Unfortunately it doesn't necessarily work that way. Our planet and solar system are currently moving through an area in our galaxy – the Photon Belt - where high frequency energies exist. This is a particular phenomenon that happens approximately every twenty-six thousand years. When this occurs we are exposed to intense high frequency energies that support super-fast changes within our consciousness. The Mayan Calendar indicated that this shift commenced in December 2012, and that this signified the beginning of an era of enlightenment. Cosmic storms and solar flare fluctuations support the process of consciousness evolvement. This is currently evidenced by the chaos, uncertainty and change occurring on every level in our world. It's this specific factor – the bombardment of high frequency energies on our planet – that is responsible for the ability to peel away those heavy, dense layers that are held deep within.

In the late nineties I channelled the Arcturians who specified that a time would come when our planet would be impacted by tsunami like waves of energy. This apparently is necessary and unavoidable. Another way of looking at this is to accept that on a cosmic level Earth and all who reside upon her are due for a shakeup, with the ultimate outcome being one that is intended to shift the energy frequency and vibrations to a more harmonious state, right across the planet.

One of their channelled messages stated:

> "When we say the energies are bombarding the Earth they are merely swirling around the universe. They are

swirling in the cosmos. In the process they are affecting your planet and all who live upon it. That includes your animal and plant kingdoms as well. There is nothing on your planet that can escape the swirling energies. At times these swirling energies are like tidal waves. They are huge and they come too in varying frequencies and densities. Scientifically there are many explanations for this, and we have already discussed such things as solar flares and windstorms. With these there are the changing frequencies that continue and which, in turn, generate further tidal wave effects......The energies are coming in with such a force they are increasing the vibration of all that exist upon your planet."

The ancient Yuga teachings have long held this to be a cyclical process of creation, and which has been outlined in ancient Hindu texts. Currently we are coming to the end times of Kali Yuga and are in transition, moving into significant changes on the planet. The Kali Yuga is a time of darkness, suffering and pain for humanity and the planet. As this stage ends it heralds in a new era consisting of ten thousand years of peace. The emerging Satya Yuga cycle is connected to our galaxy's movement through the vast universe, with the Earth's procession through the Photon Belt heralding the change from darkness to light, into higher frequency vibrational functioning.

However, in order to ultimately shift from the original density held within from all lifetimes there is a process that has to be adhered to. It's literally a one step at a time process. This means that jumping from Point A to Point Z in one or even a few steps at once isn't possible for the majority of individuals. In some instances it's possible to peel away several layers at a time, depending on each individual and unique situation. Some individuals carry a heavy load from all lifetimes, which results in greater effort required to shift and heal. Some individuals hold a lighter load, requiring less effort and time to shift. The process of peeling away the layers, in order to reveal the beautiful and breath taking gemstone (soul) within is very much an individual journey. No one solution or fix can be applied generically across a population.

The Learning

Just before the turn of the century I was fortunate to be visited by a group of non-physical beings from the Arcturus Constellation. They offered to be my teachers. Two conditions were applied to this offer. I was to cease reading all metaphysical and spiritual books, and also to stop attending workshops on the topic. It was easy to comply with these unusual conditions, though I was initially somewhat puzzled about this unexpected request. An added bonus was that this was a budget based education. A great deal of money was no longer being spent seeking information and answers. Instead, I was gifted regular contact with a source of wisdom and intelligence that taught me far more than I could have learned from any other source.

With a spiral curriculum of learning approach in place the Arcturians gradually built up my knowledge and understanding of energy – what it is, how it works, how it can be manipulated, how it impacts the human body, the power of healing with energy, power of the mind, and countless other topics related to the phenomenon of energy. During the time spent learning with the Arcturians I was often guided to sit completely still and upright in a chair, as though in a meditative position, for anywhere between thirty and sixty minutes. Next a continuous beam of strong energy would pour into my body, like an electrical current. I felt it surging throughout, from the top of my head right to my feet. It was a warm and incredibly relaxing sensation, leaving me feeling cheerful and relaxed afterwards. Within a few days I would feel as though I'd been run over by a Mack truck, with aches and pains all through my body. These energy surges were literally a way of releasing some of the denseness out of my body, gradually shifting it to a space of higher frequency or vibration.

These incredible energy surges supported my body's release of significant layers of stagnant energies. They were necessary, I was told, as part of my pre-birth plan was to be a clear channel for non-physical beings. In order to become a clear channel my energies needed to be of a higher frequency in order to be a resonant match for the non-physical energies that would be channelled. While this explanation sounds reasonable and straightforward I'd be lying if I said that it was an easy, painless process. It wasn't. There was a great deal of discomfort experienced, and on a regular basis. In addition, I often questioned my sanity in having signed up for this. At times it actually felt like my whole reality and understanding of reality was being broken down systematically. My sense of self and identity also felt threatened at times. On reflection, that was a strong indication additional work on trust issues was needed. And, even more evident I sensed that ego strength was slowly being diminished, which led to more bouts of self-questioning. Less ego and more acceptance were only two of the countless ways that my old self was being dissolved and crafted into something new and different.

There was a great deal of teaching and instruction from the Arcturians on a daily basis. The most significant and pivotal information shown was how energy is structured and functions at the subatomic microscopic level. From this I was also shown exactly how energy is damaged and what is needed for healing. That was the most basic foundation of my instruction. From that a great deal of information was provided, which in turn led me to research the quantum sciences in order to make some sense of the new and unfamiliar terrain I was exploring. Ultimately everything I learned from the Arcturians was explained in easy to understand ways. Additional information on this is further explored and explained in greater detail in Chapters One and Two.

The Solutions

All too often I hear a very familiar lament. This is expressed in different words, depending on an individual's situation, perceptions and needs. Regardless, there's a common theme repeated constantly. In my practice I see clients who have read the metaphysical literature, have put into practice all the suggested activities for expanding awareness and consciousness. Yet I still hear comments such as, "What is my purpose? I feel stuck. What else can I do as I'm not making the progress I need to make? How can I fully clear whatever is blocking my progress?" Or, I hear frustration that despite all the best endeavours there's still some restriction or limitation on an individual's ability to manifest or to achieve their desired outcomes.

As I mentioned previously the journey into expanded consciousness is ongoing, and most likely it appears to be never ending. However, I know that right now the potential for taking quantum leaps exists and is due to the intensity of the high frequency energies that continually bombard Earth. The non-physical beings I work with have stressed this often. Now is the time. Now is the time for letting go of all that no longer serves your highest good. Now is the time to support your body, and its energies, into a higher frequency vibration. It's time to leave the low frequency thoughts, emotions, behaviours and beliefs behind. It's time to step into the best possible version of yourself, holding a higher frequency than ever before. In doing so, then your life has the potential to be exactly as you'd hoped.

A great deal of the current metaphysical literature refers to the importance of shifting from third dimension to fifth dimension reality. What does this mean? How can it be achieved? In fact, how can it be measured? If it's measurable then what is used to gauge a successful outcome? Or, is it more realistic to forget about dimensional shifts and instead to refer to consciousness and awareness shifts instead? Is it possible to achieve a higher level of consciousness using the well-known techniques of forgiveness, detachment, gratitude, learning self-love and all those other metaphysical and spiritual practices that have been touted as essential for inner growth?

While these all have an important role to play in your inner growth and development there is actually a great deal more that can be achieved utilizing the power of universal cosmic energy. The power of the mind and heart can be used to direct the energy as and when it's needed or desired. In order to do this effectively understanding and applying energy to shift those extraneous and heavy density layers of stagnant emotions and memories also needs to be undertaken. It's a process. A simple yet powerful process of stripping away all that limits your potential, and which enables the power and truth of your soul to be your guiding force throughout your life.

Another way of expressing this is to view your functioning as a powerful soul being likened to the efficient performance of a super computer. When a computer is virus free it functions effectively, efficiently and speedily. That's the potential contained within your body and consciousness. However, due to generational patterning, ingrained cultural programs, beliefs, emotional wounds, and so on from all lifetimes there exists a genuine limitation to your ability to function to your full capability and potential.

In order to shift to fifth dimension or higher levels of functioning on a full time basis it's necessary to clear those hidden interferences or blockages that impede your consciousness growth. Generally speaking it's common to hold the frequencies of fourth, fifth or higher dimensions for a brief period before suddenly reverting to the lower dimension functioning. This is what I refer to as the yo-yo effect. Feeling the bliss and joy briefly and then suddenly being swamped with lower vibration emotions for no obvious reason is an indication of virus energy that limits your potential. There's no need for this yo-yo effect to be continued. By delving deeper, using the power of energy, mind and heart, those lower emotional states, blockages, resistances and fears can be transmuted into strong and clear higher frequencies.

My intention in sharing the information in this narrative is to support you into understanding the power of cosmic energy in creating this shift into the higher dimensions of consciousness. If you've already undertaken a great deal of letting go, forgiveness work, express gratitude, and so on yet feel there's still more that needs doing then this information might just be what you've been looking for. It may, hopefully, help your understanding expand. It may answer your unanswered questions. The suggestions and strategies supplied may provide the refinement you're seeking.

While my main focus in writing this book is about energy you will also find references to, and discussion about, other aspects that are relevant to this subject. To discuss only energy as a nebulous topic is to disrespect its impact in all areas of your life, whether those areas are mundane or esoteric. Because everything is energy, energy in its various forms, configurations and aspects are discussed at times, often to highlight a particular concern or relevant issue. Some of the information may seem to be slightly technical or theoretical. I've minimized coverage of research and research findings but in some instances have relied on it as a means of explaining and supporting the validity of the information that is shared.

I suggest you use this book as a reference resource. Take from it what is needed. Some of the information may challenge your beliefs. If that's the case then put those beliefs to one side and open up to other possibilities. Some of it may not be relevant to your own particular needs. However I ask that you have an open mind. Try some of the suggestions and strategies and allow time for the benefits to be noticed, felt or manifested. Be patient with yourself and with outcomes. All I share is whatever I've learned, experienced and found to be helpful and also beneficial on all levels.

My constant companions, the non-physical beings, are insistent that NOW is the time to shift into those higher frequencies of consciousness. You have the ability to do this. It's your journey to self-empowerment and actualization. You have embodied for this. Your soul knows this and is keen to guide you to step into higher states of awareness and consciousness. Enjoy the journey!

Chapter 1

Your next book about energy is going to be a continuation of the first book (The New World of Self Healing, 2006)**.** *This time however you will find new and deeper information on energy to share with readers. Already there are scientists who are speculating extensively in this field, though their research and speculation are not necessarily in alignment with the currently held theories and beliefs. As with all things there too will come a time in the very near future that many of the accepted scientific theories will be found wanting.*

*Your task in your writing is to simplify the meaning of energy in such a manner that the ordinary (non-scientific) individual can understand. This is not going to be as easy as it seems for you will be providing extremely complex technological information in a straight forward manner. (*Channeled information, 2006)

Most people aspire to a life that has meaning or purpose. That purpose varies from person to person, depending on a host of life experiences. In many ways life purpose is unique and real for each individual. In spite of this uniqueness there are also countless common similarities between people. The bonds of sharing, compassion, support and having similar aspirations are commonplace in all societies.

As well, regardless of differing values and backgrounds there are many commonalities between people and the societies in which they live. Darwinian Theory states that survival is the first instinct that is ingrained deeply within (survival of the fittest). In order to survive in the modern world there have been, over millennia and decades, great adaptive changes, not only to human physiology but also to the genetic structure.

It is these changes that have created the human beings that now exist on Earth. The human physiology is designed in a specific way, comprising a complex structure in order to be able to accommodate and withstand the many forces that impact upon the body. Underpinning what is believed to be basically a physical body is an energy system. It is this human energy system that creates the experience of reality and which, on another level, is used to create consensus reality.

However, it is appropriate to go back to the beginning. From my perspective the beginning relates to understanding energy and not the beginning of creation – whatever that may be. The first step involves examining the role and function of energy in human physiology. Why is energy important? How does it function? Expressed in its simplest form it's easy to blithely say that energy is energy, without ever fully understanding the underlying unifying powerful basis of this structured non-physical system. Expressed baldly it's easy to assert that energy is all that is, all that ever has been and all that ever will be. The point I'm making is that as a culture it's easy to refer to energy without truly understanding what it is and its relevance to human functioning and survival.

So, the questions to ask are: "What is energy? Where does it come from? How does it operate? Why is it important?" These questions, and others, will be explored and discussed throughout my narrative. Gaining a basic understanding of energy provides a basis for gleaning insights and answers to long held questions about the nature of reality and the possibilities that you are able to manifest once you gain deeper knowledge and understanding of its importance in your reality creation. You are part of an energy web, one that holds all of creation together. It has consciousness that drives the human species towards their potential journey of evolvement, not necessarily their destruction. Once you have that understanding and acceptance your potential will most likely exceed all expectations.

In order to do justice to the concept of universal or cosmic energy I'll be initially sharing, in an easy to understand way, research in the field of quantum science and its ramifications for your own experiences. I promise that the theoretical aspects will be covered briefly, and in a manner that the ordinary lay person hopefully understands. After that most of what I share will relate to how you can maximize utilization of this thing that is often vaguely referred to as energy.

Modern researchers working in the field of quantum science are continuing to delve into the mysteries of the universe. There are many theories that abound as to the origins of all life and consciousness. As scientists delve deeper they find there is still more to uncover. In some ways this journey back to the beginning of time is one of science's last frontiers to conquer because once having achieved greater understanding of this then all the previous scientific theories and postulations will have the potential to come together into a coherent picture of oneness.

In a nutshell, the energy I refer to holds consciousness. Consciousness is intelligence. Intelligence is dynamic. It is this dynamism that is the force or impetus for the creation of whatever reality is being experienced at a particular moment in time. Energy, as science teaches, cannot be created or destroyed. Whether this widely accepted fact is true for false is still to be determined. Energy, however, can be altered or changed. Energy is micro photons that formulate in varying frequencies and modulations. It is from the field of micro photons that reality creation occurs. Micro photons are even smaller than particles that are currently known to science. Cells, molecules, quarks and photons are all larger elements of what actually drives the nucleus or core of universal cosmic energy.

This energy is most definitely dynamic. It is living. It has the ability to be in all places at once and to feel and respond to all manner of things simultaneously, regardless of whether there is a distance of a few or many millions or billions of miles. This is basic quantum science. The Chaos Theory, a branch of mathematical science, focuses on the behaviour and responses of dynamic systems that are sensitive. This theory rose to prominence last century when it was postulated that the flapping of butterfly wings could cause a ripple effect, or impact, anywhere else in the world. It was hypothesized that subtle changes to systems that are highly sensitive could ultimately result in significant changes, often unanticipated.

It is this dynamic intelligence that holds and binds the entire universe or multiverse together. It is in and within everything that exists. There is no beginning to this, nor is there any ending – as far as is known. Because energy is ever expanding, ever evolving it cannot be contained within any structure. It cannot be limited and is a potent and most powerful force. It is this force that exists within all living creatures. It is this force that creates momentum. It creates whatever is desired or needed by both humans and non-humans alike.

Science has already explored at length the difference between humans and other species, citing intelligence of the mind as being the significant differing factor. The ability to think and to rationalize is what sets humans apart. However, do not for a moment think that trees, other vegetation and animals cannot sense or feel or that they lack some form of innate intelligence. If humans were to step out of their mind state and listen to the soul they would hear and know only too well that there is intelligence in all life forms.

What does this energy signify? Why is it within all living things? I suggest that you visualize fine mesh threads of energy, invisible to the naked eye. This energy weaves through everything. Though you cannot see it, without it you cannot exist. Though you are most likely unable to feel it, again without it you would not be able to function. It is this intelligence, this energy, on very subtle subatomic microscopic levels that weaves through the very fiber of absolutely everything. Along with this mesh or grid like structure of energy, sometimes referred to as 'string theory' by scientists, there is a continuous pulsing frequency that emits and transmits information.

Technology communication networks have been established worldwide. When information is transmitted along these networks it travels along radio waves of a specific frequency. In this way the receiver can then hear or see the information that is being transmitted. With communication networks there are certain radio frequencies that are available for the transmission of information. It is the same with this system of energy that weaves throughout the very fabric of All That Is, all that exists.

When you have a sense, as you pick up the phone, that the person on the other end is a certain person you might ask yourself how you intuitively know this. Did the thought just pop into mind? If so, where did that thought originate? Actually what happens is that through this existing interconnecting dynamic thread of consciousness there is actually transmission of information on a very subtle, microscopic level. When an individual is aware intuitively of the subtle levels there is a registering of minor energetic changes within. In this situation the registering is an indication that a message is on the way.

Because of the complexity of the human body there is a great deal of continuous information that is transmitted into and through each individual. Imagine an individual standing on his or her own. If you could see through this individual with a microscope and also have x-ray eyes you would see that person not in physical form as such. Instead you would see an individual being filled with a microscopic grid like structure, with fibers so small yet all fully interconnected criss-crossing and running in many directions.

Through this intricate and delicate highly sensitive system there would be information pulsing in and out, in many directions. There is transmission of information coming from countless sources entering and leaving an individual at any one time. The individual does not have conscious awareness of all the information that is passing through. Yet, if an individual had a particular interest in an area and some of the information passing through the grid like system connected with some of the stored knowledge held deep within the cellular level then there would be added information available. This additional knowledge would contribute to the existing storehouse of information held within that individual's awareness.

Another way of explaining this is to explore or expand upon the universal Law of Attraction. An individual has an interest in astrophysics, for example, and during the course of a lifetime of study has acquired a lot of knowledge. This has remained stored within this individual's learning or memory. The energy pulsing through this individual's energy matrix structure from all directions connects with the information that is already stored in memory. Instead of just passing through and not leaving any residual information it will actually attach to the stored memory. The Law of Attraction says that it will occur. When this individual expounds and shares their astrophysics passion with others, discussing in detail and at length a theoretical possibility this person may suddenly make a statement or two that seem far-fetched. It would seem to be new, something that had not been previously considered.

Upon uttering and exploring these new possibilities through discussion this particular individual realizes that maybe there is a new stream of thought, there is a new scientific possibility worthy of consideration. This may even result in a new theory that will be explored and proven through various research means. Most likely that individual will attribute that this possibility is related to something that emerged from his/her mind, from the thinking processes, when in actual fact it is stored and known information. The information is readily available throughout the universe, and due to an individual's interests and passion for a particular field of study the Law of Attraction had magnetized the information to that individual. From this realization further information will continue to be magnetized or attracted.

All the ever known knowledge, all the information that ever has existed is readily available via universal consciousness. It is a matter of magnetizing or attracting to the self. It is as simple as that. The information is transmitted via this delicate and intricate energy system. It is this energy system that is suspended and holds itself intact throughout everything. It goes beyond the universe that you know into other universes. It is both a transmitter and transceiver. It works on the principle of attraction.

Energy takes many forms. There is significant research evidence that explores the concept of energy in its many forms or aspects, and which can be explained relatively simply in non-scientific terms. Non-scientific terms and explanation may not be one hundred percent accurate in interpretation. Yet for the lay person it may be adequate description for understanding to take place. I believe it is not necessary to have knowledge of the complexities or fine detail of scientific analysis in order to have a modicum of understanding of energy and its functions. The concept of energy is one that can be readily explained in terms that are applicable and relevant to the average person who wishes to understand more in order to create meaningfully, particularly in regard to life purpose and significance. Nevertheless it is worthwhile having some understanding of the scientific basis around energy, as this will assist in your understanding of the underlying intention of what is shared throughout this book.

This chapter delves into the study and findings of some research into the vast and as yet still widely unknown field of energy dynamics. This is an exciting area of study, one that is incomprehensible to most people. Despite my many attempts to fully grasp concepts and make sense of their theoretical complexity I admit to failure on just about every count. Nevertheless some aspects of this specialized field make sense, are exciting and pave the way for new and further understanding of the nature of our co-created reality. While this field of study is of little interest to many people it nevertheless has far reaching implications for esoteric, metaphysical and spiritual studies. My attempts to make sense of the complexities of the quantum sciences have been to simplify as much as possible those concepts that are difficult to comprehend. Keep it simple has been my mantra throughout my own spiritual and paranormal experiences. I personally find complexity can become very confusing. Nevertheless, whatever I share, in terms of energy, mind and heart power have some basis in the quantum sciences, which is the reason I include research information wherever relevant.

Science and Energy

The study of quantum physics, quantum mechanics and quantum consciousness (quantum sciences) has become popularized and expanded only in recent times. The following are only some of the publications that I accessed due to a real curiosity about this emerging scientific field of discovery: Gregg Braden's work "*The Divine Matrix*" (2007); Capra Fritjof "*The Tao of Physics* (1999); Peter Grandics "*The Genesis of Fundamental Forces Acting at a Distance and Some Practical Derivations*" (2007); Lynne McTaggart "*The Field*" (2002) and Michael Talbot "*The Holographic Universe*" (1991). This particular field of study is, in many ways, following on from both Newtonian science and the brilliance of Einstein's and Tesla's contribution to the sciences. Tesla is quoted as having said, "If you want to find the secrets of the universe, think in terms of energy, frequency and vibration."

As with all fields of study there is a tendency within society for not only an acceptance, adherence and continuation of previously held truths, but also a natural momentum of exploration that will eventually result in the proposal of new concepts and theories. As there is this forward progression in theoretical research it is likely that earlier theories and tenets will be found lacking, inadequate or possibly even incorrect in some respects. This is perfectly natural, for as science continues its forward exploration of the universe new information continually comes to light. Another relevant publication by David Talbot and Wallace Thornhill, "*Thunderbolts of the Gods*" (2005) explores the possibility that the functioning of our universe is not dependent on the principles of gravity, as defined by Newton. Instead, Talbot and Thornhill explore a model of an electrical universe. They state:

> "From the smallest particle to the largest galactic formation, a web of electrical circuitry connects and unifies all of nature, organizing galaxies, energizing stars, giving birth to planets and, on our own world, controlling weather and animating biological organisms...... The medium for this more "holistic" view of the universe is *plasma*, a highly conductive state of matter, distinguished by the presence of freely moving charged particles."

Another relatively recent scientific interest is in the area of particle research referred to as neutrinos. Neutrinos are one of the particles that make up the universe. While they are similar to electrons they also have a significant difference. They do not have an electrical charge, which means they are able to pass through great distances without being affected by matter.

It would seem that as scientific study continues to delve more deeply into the nature of existence new information continually emerges. Information is now available on the microscopic and subatomic state of energy that less than a hundred years ago would have been pure speculation, or possibly not even considered as plausible. It is likely that the current field of knowledge will be expanded further within the coming generations due to the steady and possibly even exponential rate of research that is now occurring. Maybe, in time, there will be a significant re-writing of basic scientific tenets and theories in school texts, reflecting current innovative research.

Energy and the Human Body

My introduction to energy occurred in the nineties and the source of this information was solely from my non-physical teachers from the Arcturus Constellation. At that time I had not heard of neutrinos, string theory and waveform energy or quantum consciousness. In fact, the research I mention above has only in later years come to my attention. My interest at that time was solely on the energy model I had intuitively seen and worked with, and which had relevance to the functioning of the human body. Gradually, over a period of quite some time my non-physical teachers shared considerable basic information on energy structure at its subatomic level and its vital role in maintaining a healthy and strongly functioning body.

Starting in the late nineties right through into early this century, on an almost daily basis, I received information on energy from my non-physical teachers. Much of this was explained very simply, in a manner that can easily be understood by someone who does not have scientific training. Some of this information is contained in the following statements, which have been channelled and will be further expanded throughout this book.

"The Creator is energy. We in non-physical form are energy. You in physical form are energy. All energy vibrates. It vibrates at different frequencies and there are also distinctive modulations within each frequency. If all is energy then everything is connected and interconnected."

"With the changing energies (new energy frequencies affecting Earth) impacting upon your technologies your scientists will begin to discover new frequencies, vibrations and modulations. This will generate much interest, further research and experimentation, and it will in a way generate much excitement within your scientific community. At the same time it will also be the harbinger for gloom and doom, for your scientists will discover that many of your theories are in fact based on false premise and will be reluctant to reveal this to the world."

"The earlier histories of ancient civilizations show that there was greater understanding of energies and how they work. This knowledge was rapidly expanded into many areas in order to create a level of consciousness awareness that has not been seen on your planet for a long time. You are now at the brink of a time when it is possible to create this consciousness awareness again."

"For those who do not understand energies and for whom this is a new concept it will be difficult to grasp. You view energies as something that you use to provide a source for your technologies. It is energy that generates the power that runs your homes and feeds the information across the media and telecommunications. You have made this energy work in a certain way, but again it is only limited and you do not understand that you can widen your perceptions and understanding of this to incredible new levels if you so desire."

In the Introduction I shared that my non-physical teachers requested that I stop reading books and attending classes. In time I came to understand the reason for this was so that I could be a clear channel for their information. It certainly prevented confusion on my part, especially as I was completely unaware of scientific research and theories at that time. Interestingly, the information I received on energy and its structure is straightforward and was shown in a rather simplified manner despite its actual complexity. The inherent value of perceiving and understanding energy in this way is that it can be viewed and applied in a practical manner for healing, manifestation (creating) and maintaining wellbeing.

The basic energy structure that was shown can be described as a matrix, which is a form that is readily understood by most people. Initially I was clairvoyantly shown parts of the matrix in a two-dimensional aspect. This two-dimensional aspect was repeated in varying forms, and in time I came to see that this highlighted energy was often fractured, distorted, distended, compacted and out of alignment. These states indicated that damage had occurred within the matrix. As my comprehension of this two-dimensional structure increased I was gradually shown aspects of a three-dimensional matrix. At that time I viewed both the two-dimensional and three-dimensional matrix structure as fixed; in much the same way as the structure of a house appears to be solid.

In time the three-dimensional matrix appeared to be larger than I had originally envisaged. As well, its appearance changed from a fixed to a fluid state. Please keep in mind that my perception of this energy structure came from images that would flash intermittently yet regularly, across my psychic vision. It was not possible for me to hold a steady image in mind on demand. Rather, the images would flit into view for a relatively brief moment and then disappear. This occurred on a regular and consistent basis, continually adding to the information already provided.

The energy matrix can be described in a straightforward manner so that it is easily visualized and understood. Imagine a sheet of paper that has intersecting parallel lines drawn both horizontally and vertically. Next imagine this sheet of paper being placed in an upright position so that it can be seen only from the side. Alongside of it is another identical sheet, and then another and another, and so on. There is a small space between these upright sheets. However the space between the sheets is not empty. There are lines, invisible to the human sight, connecting the sheets. These lines intersect horizontally and diagonally, joining the many sheets together in a matrix structure.

The first few times this image flitted into my psychic vision it happened in nature. The normal act of walking along a path, or on a grassy playing field became both intriguing and unsettling. Instead of seeing a solid surface I saw matrix lines, connecting in varying directions. These were not always whole or the same size. They showed up as being broken, weakened and distorted. In fact, they were very irregular in appearance, with absolutely no consistent geometric pattern discernible. At first I did not realize this was seen via psychic vision as the images were vividly clear and strong. Just as soon as they appeared they would disappear, which left me wondering whether my eyesight was in need of intervention and treatment.

The grid lines of a healthy and strong matrix are very fine and translucent, spun like silken thread. In time I came to understand that this matrix is actually the supporting structure or framework along which energy flows. Also, this energy matrix exists in absolutely everything. It is the basis of all life and existence. I came to view this as being energy at the subatomic level, though I never became aware of an actual identification or classification label for it. To this day I'm still none the wiser and continue to view the world through this simplistic model structure and description.

Along the subatomic energy matrix I saw microscopic balls of golden energy flowing in all directions. It is this golden energy that I believe is often referred to as the *Ch'I* or *Prana* life force. It is these fine silken threads of the matrix, along with the golden balls of energy moving at an incredibly rapid rate that form the whole web of the energy field (or multiverse). The human body comprises and is encompassed within this energy matrix and is inextricably interconnected with all of creation through this matrix.

Though the microscopic golden balls of energy (subatomic particles) move at an incredibly rapid rate there appears to be order, rather than randomness and chaos, to this movement. When viewed distinctly, from a psychic perspective, the golden balls actually appear to be dancing gracefully along the fine, translucent matrix formation. On the occasions I have been privileged to see this phenomenon clearly I was completely mesmerized by its sheer beauty and harmony. It is literally like observing an ocean of dancing lights moving in a synchronistical formation. Chapter Three contains a description of two particular incidents in which I observed the energy matrix in its natural free flowing state.

In its natural, unimpeded state energy flows like waves moving gently in an undulating manner. Initially I had viewed the energy matrix structure as fixed and lacking flexibility, for that is how it appeared when viewed in a two-dimensional perspective. Even as a three-dimensional structure it initially appeared immovable. So it came as a surprise to observe energy moving rhythmically, and with that a realization occurred that the translucent structure also contained a considerable degree of flexibility and tensile strength.

In time I came to understand that all energy holds a frequency that vibrates. Sometimes energy vibrates at a lower (or slower) frequency. When this happens then matter appears to be more solid. At higher vibrational levels there is a higher (or faster) frequency, which is not visible to the naked eye. Needless to say, I found myself using the phrase 'vibrational frequency' quite often and relied on the teachings of my non-physical friends as an explanation for this phenomenon. Another way of explaining this is that vibrational frequency describes the rate at which subatomic particles and atoms vibrate. As the vibrational frequency rises to a higher level or rate it is actually closer to the frequency of light.

Again, it was only much later that I investigated the meaning of these words as applied in a physics context and found that the word 'frequency' refers to 'the rate of recurrence of a vibration, oscillation, cycle, etc; the number of repetitions in a given time, especially per second'. 'Vibration' refers to the 'motion to and fro, especially of the parts of a fluid or an elastic solid whose equilibrium has been disturbed or of an electromagnetic wave' (Oxford Dictionary).

Given that energy vibrates at differing frequencies and exists in absolutely everything it became natural to view the physical body and its energy field as a single unified energy field. In other words, it became increasingly difficult to separate the physical reality of a body from its larger energy domain or field.

The current study of science with its many areas of specialization tends to break down the larger, or whole, into smaller components. This involves considerable research at the microscopic level to determine behaviours, functioning, composition and structure of an organism. When studied in this manner the human body is viewed as consisting of only solid matter or substance, and not as an energy system. Basically the existence and functioning of an energy system is not integral to the study of sciences such as anatomy and physiology, and especially not in the field of western (allopathic) medicine sciences.

It required a considerable shift in my perception to accept that there was more to the physical body than I had previously been taught and understood. Actually, it was a delight to view the body as an energy system, consisting of frequencies that vibrated at different levels. This way I came to see the human body, not as an erratic and separate physical entity with composite and functioning parts, but as an integrated and dynamic energy system. Once viewed in this manner it became easy to see how healing, wellness and sickness are created and also what is needed to ensure vitality and wellbeing in a holistic manner. These concepts will be explored to some extent in later chapters.

In addition to perceiving the energy matrix as the interconnecting life force that exists in absolutely everything I have also been privileged to receive further information on energy from my non-physical teachers. This information extends beyond the concept of the energy matrix.

Early in 2006 the following information was imparted.

> *"The concept of energy is one that your scientists are continually studying. They endeavour to analyse it extensively, especially based on their current theories of understanding. It is for this reason that many of your mainstream scientists will find this task unfulfilling and frustrating. In order to understand energy from a universal perspective it will be necessary to view the concept of energy outside the currently held view of time-space."*

This information was followed by a simple visualization activity (below) that further expanded on the concept of energy.

> *"Imagine for a moment that you are holding a large crystal in your hand. What do you feel? Isn't there energy radiating*

outward from it? What is this energy? Where does it come from? This energy is light energy that is stored within the crystal structure. Over time light particles accumulate within the crystalline structure. This is due to the porous nature of the crystal stone in its early formation. This porosity solidifies over time and the light energy is held compacted and concentrated within the crystal itself. This concentration of light energy then emits in ways that are at variance to the normal fluctuations and results in an almost inexhaustible supply of energy. In this form the light energy has accumulated potency that has many potential uses. Your civilization has yet to uncover this potential."

In earlier information provided I learned that crystal energy was the energy source harnessed by earlier civilizations, particularly during the time of Atlantis.

Another relevant piece of information on energy was provided in late 2005 via channelled information (see below). This, interestingly, coincides with the research of Talbot and Thornhill referred to earlier in this chapter. At that time I was completely unaware of their research findings. This information is presented in a simple form and is my summation of what was downloaded and channelled at the time. You may wish to further explore elsewhere the ramifications of this information that is shared below.

- The universe is a unified electrical field.
- The electrical frequency held is not measured as amps or wattage, as we're used to measuring and understanding electricity.
- The unified electrical field is a crystalline structure, which holds an electrical frequency. This frequency is not known to scientists. Its frequency is not yet fully measurable, but will be in the future.
- The frequency is an amplification of ancient energies encrusted within the Earth. It was used by earlier civilizations. With misuse it can create havoc (which has happened in earlier times). However, used for a higher purpose it continues to escalate to higher, finer and purer tones. There is no limit to its frequency tone.

- The highest frequency in existence (in all universes) is not set or limited. It continues expanding.
- The human DNA contains the potential for enormous expansion. DNA has electrical force, and its expansion is activated by thought.

By now it must be obvious that the scientific study of energy, though rapidly expanding, is still in its infancy. Or, conceivably its true potential and capability may actually already be known and understood by some experts in the field. It is highly likely that some of the scientific advances in this field of study are being kept from the general public. Generally, our acceptance and understanding of this wonderful free energy source is still lamentably woeful. Maybe what is already known is being put to uses that do not necessarily benefit the general population. Regardless, whatever is the case, universal energy is readily available for use in many areas of daily life. The ground-breaking work of Tesla clearly demonstrates this fact.

What does the work of Tesla have to do with energy healing, the power of the mind, esoteric studies and more? The real extent of its relevance is still to be fully determined. Regardless, I firmly know that energy medicine is the medicine for the twenty-first century. It cannot be ingested and digested as is the case with current medical practices. Energy medicine accesses and utilizes the universal energy source. Its application and uses are in a form of advanced technology that still awaits us. Ultimately it has the potential to support you in your path to wellness and to maintain you in a state of wellbeing. In fact, it has the potential to take you as far as you choose to manifest or create. Its potential is limitless, and holds the possibility of expanding the generally accepted understanding of spiritual principles. This is something that our civilization has yet to understand and come to terms with. Once you begin to understand this the challenge is then to explore its power and to use it for your wellbeing, optimal health and consciousness expansion.

Throughout my narrative you will find instances of some information sharing being repeated, though not necessarily identical. Some experiences and explanations will be reiterated, reinforced or expanded. The reason for this is that it took me years to feel fully comfortable with, and to understand, what is actually a highly complicated subject. I understand that it may be foreign or not easy to understand if you are not overly familiar with the topic of energy and its relevance and value to your life experiences.

Chapter 2

I woke the other morning with the remnants of a dream still tantalizingly close. The words "human beings are vehicles for transmission of thoughts and emotions" echoed in my mind. What does this mean? Does it mean that we merely transmit? What about reception? I believe that the two go hand-in-hand. Being a vehicle for transmission implies that thoughts and emotions are received somewhere. That being the case, what or who is the receptor of these thoughts?

Even more provocatively, what is the impact of the emotions and thoughts that are transmitted on a non-stop basis? Even in our sleep we transmit thoughts and feelings. I cannot see a large repository waiting to receive these chaotic and random thoughts being continually transmitted. However, as the universe is consciousness in motion possibly this consciousness is the receptor of the transmitted thoughts and emotions. What is the impact upon the universal consciousness of these transmissions? Where are the transmissions eventually embedded? (Journal entry, 2004)

The Instruction

The journal entry above reflects the mental questioning and rambling that were a big part of my life for a number of years around the turn of the century. Curiosity was my habitual mode of functioning at that time. This was due largely to the influx of information that was arising in my consciousness about the nature of reality, energy and the origins of just about everything. I'd arrived at a place in my life where I'd realized that there was so, so much more to humanity's history and origins than I'd previously read in books. My focus of interest was fully immersed in digging deeper into exploring and learning about universal and galactic origins.

As a young child I had spent hours looking into the starry night, mesmerized by the stars and constellations. On a deep inner level I knew my origins were out there in the inky darkness and often I yearned to go home, back to my galactic roots. As life with all its attendant responsibilities took over that deep seated yearning was suppressed and forgotten. It was not until the early nineties that it once again resurfaced. Not surprisingly I became perplexed and intrigued to know more. It was this strong desire that resulted in the manifestation of a reconnection with non-physical companions, and which then resulted in further learning opportunities. From the early nineties I was fortunate to connect with numerous non-physical beings who provided guidance and insight into life and life's innumerable issues. It was not until I connected with a group identified as Arcturians in 2000 that my education into the imponderables intensified.

My non-physical teachers from the Arcturus Constellation were not what could be considered traditional or even normal instructors. Communication was undertaken telepathically, often at the most unexpected and inconvenient times. Occasionally I was able to see them, or their form, clairvoyantly, especially in the early stages of our connection. Once I had adjusted to their regular presence in my life it was more a case of sensing their energies, or energy signature, that alerted me to the fact that further tuition would be forthcoming. By 'energy signature' I mean that it was possible to feel or sense their presence, which had a distinct sensation as it connected with my body via the energy field. By this stage in my journey of awakening and channelling I'd come to recognize the distinctly different sensation belonging to each group, or individual, of non-physical beings that would make their presence felt.

The Arcturians were not loquacious. Far from it. In fact, the amount of words communicated telepathically by these beings was extremely limited and sparse. Having trained as an educator my familiarity with teaching was straightforward. To my mind it was merely a matter of presenting information, followed by discussion and then application of the concepts covered. Understanding would then occur either with regular practice or by linking previously learned concepts to the new information.

That was not the case in this intense, protracted and varied instruction.

There was absolutely no routine established and explanations were not conveyed telepathically in the majority of instances. The process of deduction was the main method by which my learning was acquired. In many instances I would clairvoyantly see what was needed to be seen and then mentally I began to connect that particular piece of information with other bits of information that had been previously encountered. At times I was shown unfamiliar and complex detail and would immediately seek clarification. All my questions were answered simply with words such as, "You will see. Trust. More to come" Naturally this would leave me both extremely puzzled and frustrated. In time however I came to view the mastery of this teaching as priceless.

Through practice, repetition and working gradually from basic into complex concepts I realized that the Arcturian teaching, while appearing to be simplistic, actually cleverly covered complicated and difficult concepts. In many instances awareness and understanding would eventually enter my consciousness in a nanosecond, a fraction of a second. In that nanosecond it would feel as though a massive amount of information was spewed into my awareness. While I could clairvoyantly see and even understand it all there were often instances when my ability to articulate that understanding was seriously limited or inadequate. This was due to the unfamiliarity of what was presented, along with my inability to describe with precision what made sense even though it was not necessarily what would be considered normal or commonplace in our world reality.

It was the Arcturians who regularly guided me to sit still, as though in a meditative space, for anywhere between thirty and sixty minutes at a time. During this period of absolute stillness I received massive energy infusions that would pour through the crown chakra and would fill my body completely. It felt like a warm, tingly electrical current was coursing through my body. It was very relaxing while simultaneously being stimulating to my system. This energy infusion consisted of high frequency energy, administered in doses that my physical body could tolerate, and which supported my own shift into higher frequencies. This arrangement continued intermittently, though still quite regularly for two to three years, before dwindling to regular less intense upgrades which continue to this day.

There was a purpose to this, which initially I was unaware of.

Eventually, however, the frequency of my body was sufficiently high to match or connect with theirs on some level. This enabled me to channel their messages and information while in a trance state in a more accurate and effective manner. Realistically my personal energy frequency has not ever reached the stage where it perfectly matches that of the Arcturians or other non-physical beings. However, eventually it became sufficiently high so that somewhere between the Arcturian high frequency and my not-so-high frequency an energy match or resonance occurred. It is this frequency resonance that enabled me to channel their information for longer periods than just a few odd minutes here and there. In addition it greatly aided my understanding and the wider applications of their instruction.

Prior to my communications with the beings from the Arcturus Constellation I had consistently encountered numerous non-physical beings from elsewhere for some years. It had become commonplace to sense and psychically see non-physical beings in my healing practice and in other daily situations. As well, their presence was evident in other ways. The guidance provided assisted greatly with inner growth and understanding in many areas of uncertainty in my personal life. In most instances these non-physical beings held a distinctive energy frequency, one that I was able to discern readily as a means of identification. This meant that a rapport and trust would develop over time, thereby enabling a feeling of comfort and acceptance of the higher wisdom that was imparted, as and when needed. There was never any sense of imposition or control exerted in these situations.

It is a common experience in our culture to sense the presence of departed loved ones who often make their energy felt, frequently as a form of reassurance that there is life after death and that the soul is eternal. These discarnate beings have never been my non-physical companions. I have never sought them and they have very rarely made their presence felt. Instead, my connection has consistently been with extra-terrestrials or aliens as some people call them. I view them as intelligent consciousness and have always found their discourse to be invaluable to my personal and professional journey.

The arrival of the beings from the Arcturus Constellation heralded a significant shift or change in my life. Prior to this my learning had been more of a subjective and self-focused nature. I had been privy to wisdom, guidance and information that assisted and supported my inner growth and limited understanding of the nature of life, reality and existence. It was very personal and greatly needed in order to facilitate the reduction of ego consciousness and to open up to soul consciousness.

Basically I had to get my shit together. Crappy beliefs, emotional trauma and subconscious fears held me back from achieving a somewhat undefined and untapped potential. Hence there was a constant presence of non-physical teachers who were essentially my personal life coaches for quite a lengthy period of time. These non-physical beings were wise and provided explanations and also responded to my countless questions. Communication occurred through mental telepathy. I heard voices that responded to my need for reassurance and further learning. Not once was I berated for mistakes or errors in judgment. I simply had life experiences and from that learned whatever needed to be learned, and from that greater understanding also occurred as needed. There was gentle guidance as often as it was necessary. Despite their calm support and teachings I was my own harshest critic. I pushed and demanded high expectations of my learning. At this particular stage of my personal growth I was privileged to have three non-physical beings as personal tutors. I recognized each of them by their individual energy signature. Each time one came near I felt their vibration as a tingling sensation to the right side of my body. What was interesting is that no two tingling sensations were identical and I came to recognize each of them by their particular energy vibration signature.

The unexpected appearance of a group of beings from the Arcturus Constellation heralded a major shift from the personal to the broader spectrum of consciousness. Maybe my personal learning and growth had finally reached a stage of adequacy. Possibly it was time to graduate to another level of growth potential. The Arcturians provided a bigger picture perspective. The tuition was no longer about me, my issues or my personal growth. It was time to engage the cerebral matter and attenuate it to new learning paradigms and patterning.

Surprisingly, at the time I found them to be demanding and hard task masters. My work load increased exponentially and the learning experiences were intense and consistent. It was not until much later when upon reflection, I realized the full importance of their teaching. Nowadays I refer to them as the master healers of the universe, and do so with reverence and love in my heart. It was a blessing to have endured their strictures, their convoluted teaching and especially to fully comprehend the extent of their patience and the gift that was bestowed.

As with all connections and communications with non-physical beings there comes a time for a completion or ending. In my life journey this has become a regular aspect of growth and awareness. This ending was subtle and gradual. Initially I missed their tuition and encouragement greatly. I felt their absence of spiritual guidance deeply once our soul contract had ended. Their gift, however, remains firmly etched in memory and is regularly remembered and practiced in everyday life. The basics of energy and energy healing remain entrenched in my mind and are applied when and wherever needed. Since their departure from my life I've encountered other brilliant non-physical teachers, some have added to my understanding of energy and others have diverged into different areas of knowledge. The learning opportunities presented are continuous and never ending.

The Energy System

As mentioned sketchily in the previous chapter, the human body consists of an extensive and intricate energy system. In the initial teaching provided by my teachers in non-physical form I originally became familiar with four levels of energy that are held within the human body. For convenience it is easy to simply categorize the energy system into these four basic levels – physical, mental, emotional and spiritual. When explained in this manner it simplifies understanding of how each level functions and its particular purpose. While this may appear basic it actually isn't the case. There is far greater depth and intricacy to the human energy system than even imagined or described in this book. However I will begin by sharing what I learned at the commencement of my instruction.

When approached logically each level makes sense to the average person's thought processing. Realistically though, those with a scientific inclination would find this explanation highly naive and unworkable in terms of known quantum scientific theory and applicability. The reality, however, is that most people are not scientifically inclined and often seek easy-to-understand explanations for phenomena that are outside their everyday experience. Hence, it makes sense when initially encountering a new subject area to seek a relevant and applicable model for understanding. In time, as integration of new learning occurs it is then not only relevant but also desirable to expand the acquired knowledge base to incorporate more complex concepts and material.

Below is a relatively brief summary of the four energy levels as my teachers from the Arcturus Constellation initially taught. The relevance of the four levels is today as obvious as it was at the time of their instruction. As I became familiar with and understood these levels I was steadily guided to new knowledge about the human energy system and will be exploring this additional information further in its various manifestations throughout this book.

Physical Level

The physical level is straightforward as it relates to all aspects of the functioning of the physical body. The motor mechanics of movement and all related aspects of physiological functioning can be categorized as being on the physical level. You have incarnated into a physical body that exists and interrelates within a physical and energetic world. The physical body is the vehicle for your spiritual expression, and it is your responsibility to ensure its optimal health and functioning. There is a great deal that can be done to support the physical body and to ensure that its vitality and wellbeing are of a consistently high level. Energy factors relating to the area of physical health will later be discussed, where relevant.

However, the important factor to be mindful of is that there is no separation between the physical and energetic aspects. The two are interlinked and intertwined. The physical body cannot exist without its energy component. What happens in the physical body also occurs energetically. What happens energetically also eventually impacts the physical body. It's easy to think of the physical body as having an energy field surrounding it. This is often referred to as the aura. The truth is actually the opposite. You are an energy consciousness and this hosts your physical body.

Because of the fact there's no separation, with your energy consciousness being dominant in this particular partnership I'd suggest that it's highly important and necessary to take the very best care of it and to treat it with the highest of respect and mindfulness.

Later I explore the limitations of western (allopathic) medicine, which is focused on and largely treats the physical body only, giving limited credence to spiritual, mental and emotional factors.

Emotional Level

The emotional body, like the mental body, is psychically viewed as being outside the physical body and has its basis in human emotions, which are stored from all lifetimes. It is the level at which you respond and react instinctively to situations based upon conscious and subconscious beliefs and perceptions. All emotion comes from thought. Without initial thought there can be no emotion. In many instances it is the emotional energy body that is immediately evident to the observer, especially as the energetic emotional body is located close to the physical body. For example, the emotional state of an individual is evident when there is suppressed or stored emotion. Such instances of deep grief or intense anger are immediately discernible. An observer senses (or feels) the intensity of that emotion, regardless of whatever else is occurring during conversation or interactions. The emotional intensity held by anyone is usually the immediate energy that is felt by others, and is often the basis upon which an instinctual impression of a person is gleaned.

The study of non-verbal communication has shown that approximately ninety-seven percent of your reaction upon meeting someone or hearing them speak is based upon the non-verbal cues that are emitted from that person's energy system. Hence it's easy to pick up on someone's mood, or vibe as it's often called. That particular individual may be saying one thing though the non-verbal messages being emitted may be the exact opposite. This is why it's always important to trust your first instinctual response. The energies, or vibes, don't lie. It's also important to be aware of the emotional energy you are emitting, and where possible to heal whatever unhealed emotional trauma you are holding onto. As you come to understand the complexity within your emotional layer you'll also develop skills and adaptability at transmuting those heavier emotions that lower your particular energy frequency and which most likely are inhibiting your personal growth, awareness and feelings of inner peace.

There are many ways of healing emotional pain and trauma. There are varied and different kinds of therapies readily available. Metaphysical healing opportunities and self-practice skills abound. This is the lifetime for inner growth and expansion potential. The only person who can ensure that your journey into optimal wellbeing progresses at a pace that is relevant and appropriate is you. The only person who has responsibility for healing emotional wounds you still hold is you. This is where self-empowerment and self-responsibility are important.

Mental Level

The mental body relates to thought processing and functioning. All aspects of cognition can readily be subsumed into the mental energy level. Within many cultures, especially western societies, it is highly accepted that the ability to think, reason, analyze and synthesize are highly important to existence and growth. However, ancient teachings refer to the importance of thought and its powerful ability to create. This aspect of thought, as a creation mechanism, is often overlooked in current cultural values. Thought is energy. It is an extremely potent energy and in recent times there has been a great deal written in metaphysical literature about reality creation, intention and manifestation.

All reality is created from thought, which exists and functions at the mental level of your energy system. Later I will be exploring the concept of mind expansion, as taught by my non-physical teachers. Also, the ability to use the mind for a higher purpose will be discussed and highlighted. This will assist you in shifting from much of the mental chatter and confusion of the mind, and support you into a state of enhanced wellness and higher consciousness.

In some instances it is the mental layer that is overly heavy or predominant. Instead of emitting a heaviness of emotional trauma and pain the energy of a mental dominance tends to be cool to the senses. Energetically I feel a strong, almost impenetrable barrier whenever I meet an individual whose mental energy body is overloaded. By this I mean that all their functioning, all their responses to life situations are filtered through the mind (mental body). This may be due to conditioning factors or it may be a self-protective mechanism originating from their subconscious memories. When dealing analytically with life's challenges it becomes easier for some individuals to rationalize instead of having to deal with emotional responses and issues. An emotional yo-yo response system can become energy draining, whereas dealing with issues from a mental perspective can feel safer and more comfortable for some individuals.

The concept of mental health and mind will be further explored in later chapters, more from a medical and metaphysical perspective. This is a topic that in and of itself is worthy of a whole book and would require volumes of research. It is not my intention to cover this topic to anywhere near that extent. However, to ignore it would be neglectful and disrespectful as the mental mind aspect of the energy system is pivotal to wellbeing, health and manifesting.

Spiritual Level

The spiritual, or etheric, level is not as easy to define or delineate. It does not sit alone, like a self-contained unit. The energy of the spiritual level (or body) weaves and meshes throughout the other three levels and extends beyond those levels. Its energy permeates all aspects of your existence and so therefore is evident and functioning in all levels, providing you have undertaken inner growth and spiritual work. If, on the other hand, you live life based solely on physical needs, emotional desires and mental gymnastics then there will be little or no evidence of spiritual awareness within the other three identified levels (or bodies). This does not mean that the spiritual aspect or level dies off or disappears. It simply means that it is not stimulated, expanded or honored. In some ways this results in a process of atrophy. What is ignored or lacks value cannot be cultivated or thrive in any way.

I deliberately use the word 'spiritual' in its broader context. It is part of the larger energy field and in no way connects with or is defined by any particular belief system. I use the word spiritual more for general understanding.

The Totality

Realistically there is considerably more to the human energy system than the four easily identified, simplistic and understandable levels described above. Writers and teachers have described the human energy system in varying ways, though ultimately there appears to be some degree of consensus as to the actual composition of the human energy system. There are differing layers of energy that radiate and emit outwardly from the physical body, and each layer has a specific function. The labelling that is given to each layer is more for explanation of purpose rather than anything else.

Esoteric teachings usually identify the energy system as comprising seven layers of matter and substance. The layers below are taken from Torkom Saraydarian's body of work *New Dimensions In Healing* (1992). His book provides great detail and depth of each of these levels and how they function. The levels he describes are:

1. Physical-Etheric Body. The physical aspect of this level is self-explanatory. The etheric body refers to the electromagnetic body that exists within and around the physical body.
2. Astral Body (emotional body).
3. Mental Body. The mental body is the bridge between lower and higher consciousness.
4. Fourth Cosmic Ether or Intuitional Plane (relates to blessing and pure reason).
5. Third Cosmic Ether or Atmic Plane (relates to purpose and peace).
6. Second Cosmic Ether or Monadic Plane (this plane relates to will).
7. First Cosmic Ether or Divine Plane. This plane symbolizes the Divine and/or Universal Life.

The last four planes (numbers 4-7) described above are all planes or levels of higher consciousness and from the instruction I've received from the Arcturians I believe they can be encompassed within what is described earlier as the fourth level (spiritual).

The human energy system has been described as a Seven Layer Auric Body System by Barbara Ann Brennan, *Hands of Light* (1987). Her ground breaking work is well recognized worldwide, and is often used as a reference source by energy medicine practitioners. The layers in this model include:

1. Etheric Body (this shapes and anchors the physical body).
2. Emotional Body (this interpenetrates the etheric and physical bodies).
3. Mental Body (contains the structure of thought forms).
4. Astral Level (the layer of relationships).
5. Etheric Template Body (contains the template form for the etheric layer).
6. Celestial Body (emotional layer of the spiritual body).
7. Ketheric Template or Causal Body (mental level of the spiritual body)

This model also refers to an additional two layers, and these are associated with two chakras located above the head. At the time of writing the author of this model was unable to identify the specific functioning of each of these two layers. Nevertheless, she identified a healing purpose and technique for the eighth layer.

In truth, knowledge and understanding of the human energy system functioning continues to evolve. The sources of this information are not necessarily found in scientific or technical manuals. There is no hard core data to substantiate, validate or verify the assertions of those who claim to see the structure of the human energy system. However, what is happening globally is that there is a gradual shift in consciousness occurring worldwide. More and more people are becoming aware of the non-physical and other world realities. There is greater acceptance and understanding that there exists a significant reality that is non-physical and which plays a real and major role in as yet unknown ways in daily life. People are interested in, and desirous of, knowing more about this reality.

The learning experiences I have with my teachers in non-physical form emphasize the structure of the human energy system rather than the layers of the human aura. This means that I see and describe the whole energy system as one, rather than delineating the separate and interconnecting layers. I am not sure of the reason for this, other than that seeing the whole human energy system as being part of the larger energy domain may have some, as yet unknown, relevance.

Since initial instruction of the four levels occurred there has been further instruction in relation to the functioning of the human energy system. This learning continues through the work I have undertaken with clients as well as via lucid dreams and meditations. In my earlier book, *The New World of Self Healing* (2006) I referred to the spiral curriculum approach to learning. This is the approach that my non-physical teachers used consistently.

The tuition provided by them was somewhat unusual and erratic in nature. Experiential learning is an ideal way to develop new skills and sound understanding. In my situation I often felt as though I was flying by the seat of my pants because new learning would occur on the spot, with no forewarning or notice given. Whenever there was new learning to experience and integrate there was an influx of clients presenting with similar conditions or symptoms. As I explored the specific conditions I was shown (psychically) what was happening to the human energy system and also within the physical body. Then, when it seemed I had developed some understanding and possibly even mastery of that particular symptom or condition there was another influx of clients exhibiting a different set of symptoms or conditions. Gradually and usually over a lengthy period of time, there was increasing complexity and multiplicity of symptoms evident in clients' conditions. Eventually I began to recognize and understand the pattern and explanation of what was occurring energetically.

The next chapter provides information about another aspect of the energy system. I refer to this as energy constriction. It was revealed unexpectedly and with great clarity when working with a new client. Actually, a number of clients in a very short space of time clearly demonstrated that there is greater complexity and depth to the human energy system than I could ever have envisaged initially. This new-found aspect is one that I believe many people hold within their energy system. It cannot be labelled as a level. It is more a condition that exists within the energy system, especially where there's been tension, stress or damage in some manner. Once I became aware of this I began to understand this aspect or condition as being inherent within the energy system for a reason. In some instances it serves a purpose. In other instances I realized that energy constriction impedes the healthy functioning of individuals, and could most likely have a long term impact.

Chapter 3

I found myself elsewhere, moving slowly while taking in my surroundings. It felt as though I was floating way, way out of my body. Finally I encountered a barrier or wall and had the choice as to whether I enter or remain in the current space. The choice was mine totally. Without any fear I found myself entering another space. Immediately I sensed a difference. It felt soft, inky and velvety black. Amid this was deep purple and behind that at times golden light. It was difficult to describe exactly how it was as it was totally different. Yet somehow I knew that I had connected with the Void. Here I felt the gentle pulsing of all consciousness. It moved to and fro. I sailed blissfully along it. The pulsing was within and around me. I was fully part of it and found it to be extremely deep and peaceful. This was a place where I could spend a lot of time.

The Void is written about as the web of life, the grid that holds everything together. Reluctantly I found myself leaving it, having quietly been told that it was time to depart. Once out of the Void incredible peace and calmness were experienced. At this stage I connected with an energy being who shared that the Void is a place that can be connected with at any time. It's a place of restoration and oneness. (Meditation, 2004)

Constricted Energy

In the previous two chapters I described the energy body, or system, as it had been shown psychically to me over a number of years. Whenever I would think of this energy phenomenon I visualized or saw a matrix grid structure, somewhat like that depicted in the movie *The Matrix*. Yet my understanding is that it has more complexity and depth of functioning than a basic matrix. Initially when I became aware of this matrix structure

I viewed it as a framework that holds tensile strength, meaning that while it was highly sensitive it was also somewhat fluid and flexible. In time I came to realize that the microscopic golden balls that I saw moving rapidly are, in fact, the intelligence aspect of energy while the matrix structure provides the actual framework support. Without a strong, healthy framework support the energy movement would become blocked, constricted and eventually stagnant.

Initially I viewed the matrix as simply a structure or formation upon which everything exists. However, nowadays I intuitively view the human energy matrix as actually being a hologram. This concept erupted unexpectedly into consciousness some years ago when I referred to the matrix as a hologram without having this prior thought. This, of course, sparked my interest because previously that concept had not surfaced into awareness. What I came to see and sense is that the energy matrix/hologram exists in absolutely everything and is not static or rigid. It is fluid, continually moving like gentle waves on a lake when there is no wind to create a disturbance. It is literally energy in constant motion and communication, and can be referred to as wave form energy. A couple of situations clearly demonstrated this remarkable phenomenon when I was least expecting anything unusual to happen.

About fourteen years ago, on a chilly autumn day, I was walking my dog through the streets of our neighbourhood and I came to the end of a cul de sac. This was part of our normal daily walk routine as we headed to a path that led into the woods where my dog loved to run and explore. As I neared the end of the cul de sac I immediately noticed two unusual things. Firstly, a snake approximately twelve inches in length was lying on the asphalt in the middle of the street. At that time of the year the weather conditions in the northwest of the United States are rather cool and it was not common to see snakes lying in the middle of any street. The day was certainly turning out to be interesting!

Secondly, as I was marvelling at this quirk of nature I suddenly realized that the road had disappeared from my vision. Instead of solid asphalt I clearly saw energy swirling, moving gracefully and gently. It was light and translucent. The road no longer seemed solid. It appeared insubstantial. Immediately I turned around and looked behind me and saw a regular road surface. Then I turned back and again looked up towards the end of the cul de sac and once more observed the fluid energy flowing smoothly. Needless to say the whole scene appeared surreal and I accepted that I had been privileged to observe the subatomic composition of matter. It took a while to reclaim my normal and natural three-dimensional vision and when this occurred the road reverted to its usual and anticipated bland appearance.

Not long after this incident, in a communication with my non-physical teachers, I was reminded that everything is motion, and that the universe is consciousness in motion. It should be noted that consciousness does not mean awareness. It actually denotes a level of presence or being.

Another incident occurred in December 2006 when I was traveling in the southwest of the States, as part of a book tour to celebrate the release of an earlier book. At that time I was a passenger in a vehicle, quietly relaxing and enjoying the stunning scenery. Suddenly the scenery seemed to be obliterated by a mass of movement. This movement was bright and twinkling and was all around the vehicle. It actually felt as though the vehicle was moving into this bright, swirling, twinkling mass in a similar way that vehicles drive through rainy weather conditions. The closer I looked the more I could see of the energy matrix as it bobbed up and down with the golden energy balls moving at an incredibly fast rate in all directions. The vehicle was totally immersed within this mass of moving energy. Needless to say I felt childlike delight in experiencing this occurrence. Again, there was a surreal aspect to the event. Time, space and matter seemed to be in a state of suspension, yet the experience seemed to last a long time. I was entranced by the opportunity to yet again observe the movement of energy so clearly and explicitly. My companion at the time was observing the road and scenery and was not a participant in this experience.

Both these incidents clearly demonstrated and cemented my understanding that nothing is actually solid, and that everything is really composed of subatomic microscopic energy matter that is intelligent and dynamic. Another relevant aspect appears to be the cohesion and coherence of energy particles. Energy seemingly knows what to do, how to do it and when, meaning that in some way there exists an extensive and intricate means of communication. Its intelligence, or consciousness, must surely be incomprehensible to ordinary minds!

Research by physicist Alain Aspect in 1982 in the field of quantum physics demonstrated that subatomic particles, under some circumstances, are able to communicate with one another instantaneously irrespective of whatever distance separates them. This information was shared in greater detail in Michael Talbot's book, *The Universe As A Hologram*.

The waves of energy I observed have, in the study of quantum physics and quantum consciousness, been referred to as 'waves of potential' that are transcendent (meaning beyond matter). This indicates there is a connection that occurs outside time and space in order for instantaneous communication to occur. This fact was shared by Amit Goswami in *The Self-Aware Universe*.

It is important to keep this awareness in mind when considering the functioning, importance and effectiveness of the human energy matrix/ hologram. It is not separate from the larger universal energy field. It is connected and interconnected on all levels. It contains the same properties and potentials. To further reinforce the concept of interconnectedness, whatever happens within the human energy hologram is felt elsewhere within the larger universal energy domain. And, of course, the reverse also applies. The impact of whatever occurs within the larger universal domain has an immediate impact upon the individual energy hologram, especially as communication (transmission of information) can be, and is, instantaneous.

Some time ago I encountered the statement, "Science is about proving and disproving theories", and I believe that the source of this statement may actually have come from a scientist. That particular statement presents the study of science in a very different perspective. For far too many years I've been under the assumption that what was scientifically proven must be a fact, when in reality scientific proof really means that a theory has been proved, and that proof remains in place until another theory disproves it. I am sharing this perspective so that you will also have a clearer understanding of the underlying basis of all scientific research and facts. They are fluid, open to interpretation, understanding and change. Basically nothing remains constant in our knowledge and understanding of life, reality, science and phenomena.

Having shared the above statement about science I'm not about to debunk scientific methodology. Science has contributed inordinately to our understanding in countless fields of research. In scientific research experiment conditions are controlled, meaning that it is common for a perfect or ideal situation to be studied and analyzed. Once a baseline or standard has been clearly identified within a condition it is then subjected to external factors in order to measure response or reactions. Basically, in a controlled experiment conditions are ideal or as near to perfect as possible.

When I observed the wave motions of the asphalt on the road and also when traveling through the larger energy domain it seemed that I was observing the perfection of energy in motion. It was moving freely and in what I assume to be a very ordered and structured manner, though it may actually have appeared as being chaotic. I consider these sightings as being the baseline for my understanding of the energy subatomic particle framework. By this I understand and consider that freely and rapidly flowing energy is the ideal state. There are no blockages, constrictions, distortions and so on to impede not only the flow, but also the communication (or transmission) of information.

This ideal baseline is not what I generally see, sense or feel in clients when undertaking energy medicine work. Rather, it is normal to encounter energy blockages, imprints and constrictions in various parts of the human energy hologram. All these indicate that there is some discomfort, dis-ease or illness manifesting on some level for the individual, especially when there has been a significant level of interference to energy flow for considerable time.

It has only been in more recent years that I became aware of the existence and impact of energy constriction upon the health of an individual. The word 'constriction' aptly describes exactly what I see and understand it to be. According to the Oxford Dictionary, 'constrict' means "to make narrow or tight; compress and cause organic tissue to contract".

The first time I encountered this specific situation with a client I immediately felt the energy hologram as being close to the body and rigid in structure rather than being fluid and expansive. When I scanned the whole body I found this to be the case throughout. Intuitively I knew this client actually lived with constant inner tension that also would have resulted in tight muscles throughout her body.

Gradually I came to see more and more clients exhibiting this constriction. In one case I intuitively sensed that the constriction commenced when the foetus was in the womb. The developing foetus felt the energy of tension between her parents. Regular and intense arguing by the parents was like a barrage or assault upon the sensitive energy system of the unborn child, resulting in the inward contraction of energy. This inward withdrawal can be likened to a self-preservation mechanism, so that the energy hologram formed a protective shield, which was carried into physical life and affected her health and life on many levels.

Though my work is not of a scientific or medical nature my intuitive understanding has identified some physical conditions that may be linked to, or caused by, energy constriction. They include hypertension, migraines, tight muscles and poor proprioceptive awareness. The individual experiencing energy constriction may feel tightness within the body, may feel less fluidity and freedom of movement. It is also likely that there will be a constant feeling of inner tension and sensitivity to loud noises, intense emotions and discordant energies. Constriction may also result in a reluctance to take risks in life. It may contribute to a need to be in control of life situations, where subconscious fears determine the necessity of living safely at all times and in all situations.

Constriction can also occur suddenly, and can be caused by factors such as an accident or great fear of some unknown issue or situation. In such instances when an individual has a strong constitution, healthy self-esteem and functions mainly from a positive outlook or perspective on life the constriction will most likely gradually heal and the energy hologram may revert to a healthy state.

In many instances individuals with constricted energy will seek relief and healing from various practitioners. When I encounter clients with energy constriction it is normal to hear them say that they have been regularly receiving massage therapy, chiropractic corrections, physical therapy and other healing modalities. In most instances the therapies would temporarily alleviate the discomfort being experienced but would not necessarily heal the underlying problem. In time I came to understand that lasting healing would only ever occur when the energy hologram was healed and expanded to its natural state. Optimal healing takes place once the energy hologram reverts to an expanded and fluid state.

This may be one explanation for why some people seem to take forever to heal, even when regular and quality therapy is undertaken. Energy constriction has to be healed first before healing on other levels can occur.

An analogy to best describe the above situation is what happens to water flowing through a waste pipe. When the pipe is new water flows freely through it. Over time however debris, sludge, chemicals and other matter build up inside the water pipe. This build up may eventually become pronounced thus forcing the flow of water to a trickle. The flow has become constricted. No longer is it fluid and free, it merely flows erratically and slowly; and is hampered by the limited space it now has available to move through. The water will not be able to flow freely until the matter constricting and limiting its movement is completely cleared.

It is the same with the energy hologram. When in its expanded and natural state energy flows freely, creating wellness and balance. When it is constricted there is limitation on different levels and gradually, over time, there is a depletion of vital life force leading to discomfort and illness on the physical, mental and emotional levels.

Healing Energy Constriction

The information above contains an explanation of energy movement in its natural, expanded state. This state is indicative of wholeness, vitality and unimpeded functionality. As was also shared, while this state is an ideal it is not always necessarily what actually occurs, especially in the human energy hologram. In fact, if you've been injured in a sporting or vehicle accident it's likely that there's been some constriction, limitation or distortion in your body's energy flow. A single accident may result in minor distortion. A lifetime of injuries presents a very different picture.

Imagine an energy hologram without constriction. You will visualize the energy flow being free and unimpeded, supporting a healthy body. Compare it with a body where energy constriction has occurred, due possibly to emotional stress, abuse, sporting injuries or accidents. In this instance it is most likely that an individual with this narrowing and squeezing of the energy grid framework has less fluidity and flexibility within his or her body. It is also likely that this individual experiences feelings of being tense, on edge and may even feel nerves tingling continuously within the body.

Constriction of the energy structure occurs for numerous reasons and in various situations, which often become more apparent as the years roll on. An individual experiencing continual tension and tightness within their body and not understanding or being able to rectify the situation must at times feel frustrated.

Some years ago a client came for a session, seeking to have her energies balanced. This client had been experiencing digestive problems since she was a small child. As I began working with her energies I immediately saw a distorted and constricted energy structure. Her whole energy hologram had tightened inwards, as though the vertical (north-south) grid lines were spaced much closer than I normally encounter. While working to straighten and expand her energy structure I psychically saw a young child being buffeted by gale force winds, which were coming at her in all directions. This image represented her feelings of being helpless under an assault of stressful life situations. My immediate sense was that she had internalized a lot of adult reality, including anger, as a young child, and this constricted her energy system. In some way the only means she had with which to protect her young sensitivity was to withdraw inward, like a wounded child. This was done reflexively and unconsciously through the pulling inward of her energy hologram.

Often, when working with clients, I immediately sense that their nervous system is tense. When my hands connect with their energy hologram I intuitively feel the tightness, along with an on-edge sensation. It is as though these individuals live life constantly feeling stretched to the max. They experience limited relief when undertaking gentle stretching exercise such as yoga or tai chi, and even when engaging in meditation practice. In order for a constricted energy hologram to be expanded back into regular functioning considerable persistence and patience is required. As was mentioned previously, bodywork and regular exercise are beneficial for healing energy constriction. However, without additional energy expansion work recovery may often be slow, though that is not always necessarily so. It all depends on the length of time that energy constriction has been in place. An older person who is carrying a lifetime of tension and other contributing factors that induce constriction will take longer to permanently relax and release that constriction. A young person who has been involved in a sporting injury will most likely recover quickly and easily, with energy hologram functioning fully, as it's designed to do.

A poignant story emerged when working with a new client. She was an avid yoga practitioner and engaged in yoga practice on a daily basis. She came for an energy session with the hope of finding a reason for the ongoing tightness in her body, which should have released given her devotion to breath work and yoga practice. Immediately upon connecting with her energy hologram I felt massive constriction all the way along the mid-line of her body, along the spinal column. The energy felt locked in and seemed to be immovable. When I scanned her body I noticed that the whole hologram was situated very close to her body. Energetically she was closed off and tense all the way through. At that stage the extent of this constriction was the most severe I'd ever seen and felt. Intuitively I picked up on the energy of abuse, which was confirmed during the course of the session. This client had been raped as well as experiencing sexual abuse in her younger years. Instinctively her energy hologram had reflexively been pulled inward as a self-protection mechanism. The abuse she'd experienced had lasted a number of years, which resulted in her energy hologram being cemented into a restrictive and tight configuration. Overall it took several sessions before the constriction was finally relaxed and released. Gradually my client was then better able to manoeuvre her body into difficult yoga positions without distress or discomfort. Along the way she'd also fully let go of the trauma memory of sexual abuse.

When encountering a new concept in my energy healing work it is always normal practice to seek understanding and, of course, some means of correcting any energy imbalance pertaining to this new concept. This was definitely the case with the concept of energy constriction. It was not long after I had become aware of its existence that I was apprised of a possible means of healing the constricted energy structure. This information came during a meditation where I was shown that the energy matrix structure (within the hologram) consists of axes sitting within coordinate points. The solution seemed to be remarkably straightforward once I had been shown how it could be achieved. Psychically I saw that the lines of the energy matrix structure could be moved when they're misaligned or constricted. The image I saw is one that most adults remember from their high school mathematics classes.

I was shown a visual representation of the energy grid structure in a basic two-dimensional format as consisting of axes sitting within coordinate points. When there is distress to the body in some way the grid lines may move from their designated coordinate points. This can be corrected by using the mind to mentally move the grid lines back to their correct coordinate points.

In order to reinforce this concept I was guided to my own body. I had been experiencing slight discomfort and some pain along the left side of my back, near the midline of the body. The vertical gridlines were constricted and misaligned. So I mentally made the adjustments, and was guided as to which coordinates required realignment. This involved visualizing one vertical line at a time and moving it either to the right or left of the mid line, and into a position that was parallel to the gridline next to it. The process seemed to take a while, yet in reality it couldn't have taken more than a few seconds. After I came out of the meditation my back felt straight and pain free.

In my meditation I was shown the mid-line from which the grid lines were gently moved outwards from the center. This principle works whether the constriction is vertical or horizontal or both. It involves finding a mid-point from which to begin mentally straightening out and expanding the energy lines. This is all undertaken using the power of the mind and visualizing the changes. Where there is constriction in both the horizontal and vertical planes then the visualization will involve two mid-points (x and y axes). The mid-point goes through the body from the crown chakra to the coccyx. I take the mid-line for the vertical grids to be along the spinal cord. For the horizontal mid-line I use the shoulders or even the waist as a rough baseline.

Undertaking this precise restructuring of the energy framework is not difficult though should be applied only when you are fully familiar with the energy flow and structure of your energy hologram. However, in order to receive positive results it is essential to be able to meditate, or sit quietly without continuous mind chatter occurring. My experience has been that considerable concentration is required to complete this task, especially when first learning how to mentally manoeuvre the gridlines. Some people have difficulty in visualizing and it is perfectly acceptable to imagine the grid structure and also the work that is undertaken. If you are unable to visualize but able to imagine or pretend then you are capable of performing this energy correction and adjustment activity.

Another option is to visualize your body as balanced and healed on all levels. Then mentally thank your body for self-correcting the energy hologram wherever it is needed. The concept of body talk will be explored further in a later chapter. Or, if you are uncertain then I recommend that you begin with the Additional Method of Expanding Constricted Energy, described below.

The above technique may require repeating several times for the correction to hold. This is especially the case with someone who has been living with constricted energy for many years. It takes time for the energy hologram (and body) to revert to its original and balanced state. This is due to the fact that the human physical body accommodates itself to trauma it has experienced and over a thirty-day period following the trauma integrates the changes within its system. It then becomes normal for the body to work with the impact of a trauma and to set a new point for what is considered normal or balanced. Retraining the body into a new state of balance takes persistence as the body has adjusted to a different framework of balance and often relinquishes it reluctantly.

Additional Method of Expanding Constricted Energy

The above method of expanding constricted energy may be too difficult or confusing, especially if you are not comfortable with being in a meditative state, visualizing or unused to using your mind to consciously create change within your energy hologram. Another method I was shown is not as precise, though its application will certainly assist in creating clear energy flow throughout the energy hologram. This method is also applicable for clearing blocked energy. Ultimately the aim of undertaking this exercise is to create a clear path for the energy flow, which in turn facilitates healing and expansion of the energy hologram.

My teachers in non-physical form guided me to use this way of self-healing at a time when my body felt like it held countless energy blockages and constrictions. Initially it was extremely difficult, if not impossible, for the energy to flow freely through my body. Ultimately it was persistence and a great deal of repetition that resulted in the energy flowing effortlessly from the top of my head to my feet. In terms of time, it took months of diligent practice to achieve this result. However, the result was well worth the effort as it generated increased wellness and wellbeing. I felt lighter and clearer, and certainly more balanced within.

- Begin by sitting still, with eyes closed and without distractions.
- As you begin to relax focus on breathing deeply, letting go of thoughts. Realistically, thoughts will intrude. Pay no attention to them and focus attention to your breath.
- When in a relaxed state visualize, or imagine, a cylinder of golden energy coming from the universe and entering the crown chakra.
- Using your mind's eye gradually bring this golden cylinder down through your head. It goes down along the mid-line of your body. This cylinder is spinning and as it spins it radiates gold energy outwards from its centre to other parts of your body.
- Feel the golden energy cylinder as it moves all the way down the neck to the top of the thoracic vertebra (where the shoulders are located).
- If at any time you have difficulty in moving the golden energy cylinder downwards it is because you have an energy blockage. When you encounter an energy blockage just gently ease the golden energy through the blockage. The resistance may continue. Persevere for as long as you feel is appropriate and if you are unable to move through the blockage then move the golden energy cylinder to the space just below where the blockage is located and continue downwards.
- Move the cylinder (in your mind's eye) along the mid-line (spinal column) slowly and steadily. Feel any resistance move slowly to the side and dissolve as you move along. It is possible that you will encounter several energy blockages along the way.
- When you reach the sacrum move the golden energy cylinder to the right. Move steadily across to the right hip and then begin the steady journey down the right leg, to the right foot and into the earth.
- Then bring your attention back to the sacrum where you will reconnect with the energy cylinder.

- From the sacrum, move across to the left hip and repeat the process as for the right leg.
- Finally, bring your attention back to the sacrum and move the still spinning energy cylinder down through the coccyx, the intestines, colon and reproductive system.
- Now your whole body has been filled with golden light that continues to spin rapidly, sending healing energy to areas that are constricted, blocked or distorted. When ready bring your attention back to the room you are sitting in and feel the difference in your body.

This method is less accurate than the first one described. However, it works well and supports the body's natural mechanisms for self-correction and healing. In fact, I recommend that the second method be applied initially. Over a period of days and weeks the changes and improvements are subtle yet discernible. Once comfort and mastery have been achieved with this technique then you may feel comfortable with applying the more complex technique described first.

Releasing Constriction Simply

Sometimes the easiest way is the most immediate and effective. As mentioned earlier the cosmic energies impacting Earth are currently of a higher frequency due to the solar system moving through the Photon Belt. The rotation through this belt of high frequency energy has an unexpected and very helpful benefit. It enables the power of thought and intention to manifest more rapidly, certainly with more speed, accuracy and efficacy than fifty years ago.

This means that thought and intention now have more capacity for immediate and effective response. I've learned this through experience simply by observing my body's responses and the ease with which it reacts to simple statements and commands. A clearly expressed statement beginning with "I release with love…." followed by the intended outcome is often sufficient energy to generate a desired change. In the situation with energy constriction, especially when there's long term tension, it may take numerous statements over a period of time for the full effectiveness to become apparent.

As an example I would say something along the lines of: "I release with love all tension and constriction that is held within my energy hologram". In addition I would express gratitude with statements such as, "I am deeply grateful to my body for releasing stored tension and for releasing any constriction that prevents me from achieving optimal health". It's a matter of choosing words that best suit your situation. The only proviso I would suggest is for the statements to be in the present tense, with no reference to the future at all. It has to be as if it is occurring in the Now moment, not something that will happen by some predetermined date that you feel meets your needs.

Have no expectations of specific healing progress or of time limits. Your body is a living, dynamic organism. It reacts to every thought, intention and emotion. It also responds in a manner that is supportive of good healing and health and that sometimes means it takes longer than anticipated. Yet, healing always occurs in a perfect manner in the perfect timing. Your body's innate intelligence knows what is needed and responds accordingly.

Conscious manifestation relates to more than creating material possessions, healthy relationships and other tangible outcomes. Mindfully applying the power of intention has the potential to improve physical health and wellbeing, as well as supporting spiritual growth and overall enrichment of life experiences.

Chapter 4

Yesterday in meditation I went in really deep and with a purpose. I'd had a sense of what was needed to shift some of this constant leg pain. Despite all my attempts to heal on a physical level there was still a lot of constant aches and deep pain. In this deep (theta) state I commanded that the belief that it is fearful to move forward be released and replaced with an affirmative that I am fearless and able to move forward easily. When I did this I felt some energetic changes and surges. Then I found myself looking deeper into my body and found myself commanding that the cell receptors on my muscles be reversed from 'flight or fight' response to a normal mode of functioning. This too was affirmed energetically. When I came to I could still feel the energies swirling, and when it was time to stand up my legs certainly felt vastly different. They felt good and I know that something has been released.

Four days later. *Subtle yet significant changes have occurred since the healing on my legs. Immediately my legs felt wobbly though different. That anticipated difference has occurred. There are still some incredibly tight muscles that need to be massaged into suppleness. Needless, I know that something major has shifted within my body. I feel less tense. Initially I thought that the fight or flight state was the result of the horse accident in 2003. Yesterday as I was changing to go to the gym I had the immediate knowing that my body has been in fight or flight mode for many years! Now I feel less tense. I no longer feel trapped and neither do I look for opportunities to escape.* (January 2005)

Energy Imprint

The human energy system is highly sensitive and indescribably complex. Initially, when observing and feeling energy, the word 'system' seemed an apt descriptor, as 'system' describes 'a complex whole; a set of connected things or parts' (from the Oxford Dictionary). However, as mentioned in the previous chapter, in time I inadvertently and unconsciously found myself referring to this system as an energy hologram. The word 'hologram' feels more accurate and in greater alignment with the incredible complexity, depth and storage capacity of the energy field that is within and around each person. It encapsulates the whole aspect, physical body and energy body as one and not as distinct separate entities. The Oxford Dictionary defines 'hologram' to mean 'a three-dimensional image formed by the interference of light beams from a coherent light source'. This is a physics definition and explains how an image, when suitably illuminated (generally with a laser beam), produces a three-dimensional image.

Basically, a hologram reveals the whole entity or object when illuminated, even when only a segment remains. Each part or segment contains some, or all, information of the whole system or configuration. Holograms and their relevance to energy and the universe have been extensively explored and studied. David Bohm and Karl Pribram are two respected proponents of the universal hologram theory. The hologram theory dispels the concept of separateness, instead indicating that everything is interconnected via subatomic particles that communicate information at speeds faster than light.

Pribram's research into the brain and memory contends that the brain functions as a hologram. He argues that memory is encoded in patterns of nerve impulses that intersect in a crisscross fashion throughout the brain. This concept is vastly different to previous theories of memory being encoded in neurons. His theory describes the energy grid (or matrix) that is explored and described in my earlier book, *The New World of Self Healing*.

It was only when I became aware of the research relating to quantum consciousness that the reason for referring to the energy system as a hologram became apparent. The human energy system is in fact a hologram. Information stored in this super system is not segmented or compartmentalized. It is not clearly labelled or easily identified as belonging to separate aspects of the whole. For example, when working with clients experiencing emotional issues it is common to find memory relating to specific emotions in various parts of the hologram, rather than being localized within a chakra or particular part of the body. This is despite the earlier work of Louise Hay and others who linked emotional issues or concerns with specific body components.

As was discussed previously, the human body is not composed of self-contained organs, bones, and so on that function separately and in isolation from the whole. When an individual experiences pain in one part of the body its cause may actually be located elsewhere. For example, neck pain may be due to a number of physical factors including spinal misalignment, lower back problems, incorrect posture, and so on. Neck pain can also relate to metaphysical, spiritual or emotional issues from more than one lifetime. Treating the neck pain as a physical condition only and ignoring other likely causes will not necessarily result in lasting healing, instead possibly only providing temporary relief to the patient.

The interconnectedness existing in the human body is experienced and evidenced whenever an individual succumbs to an illness or health related condition. Some years ago, an acquaintance sought the skills of a doctor to remove several benign moles from her back. The procedure was straightforward and she assumed that she would be able to resume her normal routine within a day. The following day her back was in extreme pain, which took over a week to ease. Even the slightest movement caused distress within her body. This pain was due to the trauma of simple surgical procedures that impacted her nervous system, and from that the muscular system. It quickly became apparent that the minor procedure had affected a significant proportion of her body, and clearly demonstrated the extent of the interconnectedness within the human physiology.

Another common condition, gastro-intestinal digestive disorder, impacts more than just the stomach, intestines, colon and bowel. Due to the circulatory nature of the human body, both blood and lymph play a vital role in the oxygenation of cells and elimination of body wastes. When an individual has digestive problems then the symptoms of these become evident throughout the body, especially when there has been long-term deterioration. Natural therapy practitioners are able to easily see and diagnose the digestive disorders through various means, including iridology examination, feeling the energy flow, taking a reading of the vital organ pulses (Traditional Chinese Medicine), and more. In other words, whatever is happening within a specific area of the physical body reveals itself clearly in the larger body mass.

As will be discussed in Chapter Six, current medical and scientific research tends to focus on breaking down the whole into smaller components or parts. An example of this is the research into cancer, diabetes or any other major illness. A great deal of medical research is focused on discovering what happens at the microscopic level of cellular activity. It is believed that once all the evidence is revealed then science will be in a position to provide solutions to the illnesses that plague our world. While there is inherent value in having greater understanding of the mechanisms of the human organism, this approach does not necessarily acknowledge the interconnectedness aspect of the body's overall functioning.

It is this interconnectedness that is inherent within the energy hologram. This now brings me to the challenge of describing as simply and clearly as possible what this interconnectedness consists of, how it actually manifests, and how it can be corrected when there are indications or symptoms of misalignment or illness. It's a truly magnificent system, one that is beyond the scope of human imagination and creation!

Energy Hologram

The human energy hologram is an intricate storage system. It contains and retains information and memory of all that you are and all that you have ever been. This does not pertain to only this lifetime. It encapsulates and relates to all experiences in all lifetimes.

Energy medicine practitioners will often see or feel energy blockages and have an insight or intuitive knowing that a particular blockage relates to either the current life, is from other lifetimes or is a mix from all lifetimes. Often the information gleaned from the energy hologram is vivid and precise. For example, it is common to see and/or feel blocked energy around a stab or gunshot wound, a hanging, burning or some other form of inflicted physical trauma.

It is not only energy medicine practitioners that encounter other lifetime memories in the course of their work. In some instances when psychiatrists undertake hypnosis on their clients they are astounded to find their clients relating memories of other lifetimes. Surprisingly, what has been discovered is that often the root cause of current life problems or anxieties lies in other lifetime experiences and issues. These well-known instances have been recorded by Brian L. Weiss MD (*Same Soul, Many Bodies*) and Michael Newton PhD *(Life Between Lives)* and other practitioners worldwide.

In addition to the memory of physical injuries sustained there is also the memory of both emotional and mental states as well as spiritual dysfunction. For instance, an individual may have been burned at the stake in another life for practicing witchcraft or heresy. The emotions of fear - including fear of fire, fear of being persecuted, fear of speaking one's truth, and so on – remain within the energy hologram. Memory of thoughts (mental state) is retained and at the subconscious level an individual may believe that it's not safe to be different from other people, that authority figures are to be feared, and that it is safer to accept and comply rather than to question and explore.

Given the oral and written history of our civilization it is clearly evident that man's treatment of his own kind has been brutal. History records wars, battles, enmities, conflict, adversity, betrayal, and mistrust. Each lifetime experienced leaves its memory imprint within the energy hologram. This is not to say that all deep-seated memories are negative or involve suffering. However, there's no doubt some memories may impinge upon your ability to live a purposeful and joyful life. When this is the case, then it can be highly beneficial to clear and heal the memory that is creating dissonance in your current life situation.

Hologram Interconnectedness

In Chapters One and Two I describe the energy system as it was initially shown psychically and how it functions and impacts on a daily basis. As well, I provided clear descriptions of the manner in which energy moves. Energy is intelligent and has consciousness. Everything in the Universe works according to the Law of Attraction (Esther and Jerry Hicks, *Ask and It is Given*). It is the functioning of this profound and powerful Law of Attraction that creates whatever manifests within your life experiences. You are a creator and continually magnetize experiences to challenge and enhance your soul's evolvement.

As energy has both intelligence and consciousness it knows best how and what to do with whatever life issues occur. The memory of those experiences is stored within the memory bank of the hologram, in much the same way as a computer stores programming that has been inputted by a computer programmer. The more often a specific memory is stored the stronger the energy it holds. Over time the intensity of that stored energy becomes discernible to the energy sensitive practitioner, to empaths and is also discernible via non-verbal cues.

During the course of numerous lifetimes there is often a common or recurring theme that occurs. Due to your powers of attracting whatever you are feeling, thinking and experiencing there is a gradual build-up of a particular energy charge within your energy hologram. The theme you experience is yours to resolve and heal in this lifetime, if you so choose.

Metaphysical teachings attribute particular physical conditions to associated underlying emotional and spiritual causes. Both Annette Noontil, *The Body is the Barometer of the Soul* and Louise Hay, *You Can Heal Your Life* have provided significant information on this topic. When healing occurs energetically on the underlying causes then the physical condition can begin to heal. For example, when a client presents with stomach problems it is easy to explore whether there is sufficient hydrochloric acid in the stomach, or whether there is a likelihood of a stress induced ulcer, or some other possible physical explanation. However, metaphysically I also believe in exploring aspects of the client's life that he or she may have difficulty stomaching or dealing with. Usually the underlying emotional reason surfaces rapidly. When energy healing is undertaken it is common for healing to occur in the stomach region, as well as a number of other seemingly unrelated parts of the body. In some way the emotional pain manifesting in the stomach and digestive system is also located elsewhere in the energy hologram. At this time I have been unable to determine whether there is a precise pattern of stored emotional locations for specific physical conditions.

Stored Imprints

When the energy hologram holds stored memory in a particular location that relates to a specific incident or issue I refer to it as an 'energy imprint'. This means there is a clear and distinct energy memory and impression of earlier incidents, often from other lifetimes. Below are several case histories to explain and emphasize how energy imprints can affect an individual's life.

My analysis and perception of what this means in current life experiences is that these energy imprints actually weaken the energy hologram, most particularly where the imprint is exceptionally strong or dense. An example to highlight this point is that of an acquaintance I was doing energy healing work on. As my hands and eyes scanned her body I found an imprint in the lower abdomen, and psychically saw a large gaping hole in her intestines. Almost immediately I received information that the hole was from a musket shot, delivered during the American Civil War. As I shared this information she immediately commented that she now understood why her digestive system was problematic. Her energy hologram was not strong or balanced in the area of her digestive tract due to the imprinted memory stored from another lifetime.

I remember a client sharing that she consistently had coldness in her legs and feet. Over the years she had sought all manner of treatment, all to no avail. As I was working on her hologram I found that her energy flow was strong and healthy from her head to torso, and that it was definitely weak in her legs. I sought a reason for this discrepancy and immediately psychically saw that in another lifetime she had been a male. For ease of description I will continue to refer to this client as 'her' rather than the masculine 'he' identified in this earlier lifetime. It seemed as though she had been taken captive and was on a sailing vessel. The vessel looked crude and roughly hewn. The seas were rough and I saw her being thrown overboard with her legs hitting the water first. I immediately received the impression that as her feet and legs hit the water the instant chill of the water registered on some level, and the energy around her legs contracted from the contact with the icy water. Fourteen months after the session I contacted this client about the circulation in her legs. Her response was, "I don't feel the inhibiting cold in my legs the way I used to".

Another client was still at school. She exhibited an extensive array of symptoms including: pain in all joints; swelling in the feet, hands and knees; debilitating migraines; irregular bowel movements; and continual tiredness. Doctors had diagnosed depression and fibromyalgia, for which she had been prescribed medications. This young client ate a healthy diet, comprising mainly organic foods. She exercised regularly and overall endeavoured to follow a healthy lifestyle routine. Initially I was perplexed as to what could be the reason for the multiplicity of symptoms. There seemed to be no logical reason for her ill health. While pondering some possible causes I immediately saw an image of a young person, wearing clothing of a different era, being sucked into a bog or marsh. My sense was that it may have occurred in Scotland. The image was clear. This person was sucked fully into the quagmire and lost her life in that manner. In this other lifetime the bog suffocated her to death. This experience left an imprint of tightness and flow constriction within her energy hologram. After one healing session the migraines reduced considerably, the pain in the joints faded gradually and her bowel movements became regular. She was also able to wean herself off medications. The biggest improvement however was in her mental state, as she became calmer and felt more in control of her body.

The above case studies above are only a small sampling of the countless energy imprints that I have seen and felt over the years. In the physical body they present as different conditions, depending on the extent of their denseness within the energy hologram.

Imprint Impact

Initially I had been aware of only the four basic levels within the human energy hologram, as taught by my non-physical teachers. The simplistic physical, mental, emotional and spiritual levels served a purpose for developing initial understanding. In encountering energy constriction and imprints I became aware that there are other factors that have significant impact on individual functioning and health. The energy imprint aspect consists of embedded memory, which does not clearly fall into any of the other four basic levels discussed in Chapter Two. Embedded memory can contain emotion as well as thought forms, along with the memory of physical causation. Energy imprints exist within the human energy hologram and their impact upon your present life is determined by the extent of the memory stored within the hologram.

An energy imprint has the potential to weaken the human body, often resulting in several symptoms appearing in the area of its energetic location. However, as the memory of the energy imprint is healed the energy hologram and also the physical body strengthen and become more balanced. Often clients report that they continually feel a steady or dull pain in certain areas of the body, which conventional medical treatment has been unable to diagnose or heal. In such instances it may be worthwhile exploring possible natural therapies that may be beneficial.

Healing Imprints

Energy imprints can make their presence felt in various ways. To highlight just how varying they can be, below I share several examples where energy imprints became apparent and also how they were cleared. Once an energy imprint is cleared and released then the human energy hologram undergoes a process of reintegration, meaning that the area previously holding the imprint is firstly filled with light and then the matrix rebuilds itself into a whole and balanced segment once again. The reason for this is that there is no such thing as empty space in the universe. Energy will immediately flow to the empty space and instead of stagnant memory (blocked energy) the area now recovers its tensile strength. It is then clear of impediments and does not contain memory. When this occurs there is a reconnection of the energy framework structure described in Chapters One and Two.

Bodywork and Releasing

After receiving an intense massage session, I experienced some after-effects. This often happens after any form of bodywork session and involves a myriad of uncomfortable sensations occurring in the body. In this particular instance I intuitively knew that I was releasing what I fondly refer to as 'old stuff' (stored and blocked energy). In response to the massage my body was totally lethargic, feeling as though it had succumbed to a virus.

My response to feeling debilitated was to support the release and healing process. It felt natural to lie down on my back and place some healing crystals on my torso, as well as around my body. Almost immediately there was a reaction. Initially energy flowed strongly along the right side of my body, and this actually felt like worms wriggling inside.

It was uncomfortable, yet I immediately knew it indicated that energy was flowing where previously it had been blocked. Simultaneously I psychically saw myself as a young warrior with injuries sustained to that side of the body. The injury was mainly in the chest, where there was a large badly infected wound. Intuitively I sensed that sepsis had set in.

I worked intensively with the crystals to clear and release the energy imprint. This involved firstly just lying still and allowing the healing energy in the crystals to do what was needed. Next, placing my hands on different parts of the body facilitated further healing. Finally I went into a meditative state and requested that healers and physicians of the light assist with any additional healing that was required. Within approximately two hours the imprint lifted off my body, leaving me feeling clear and drained. After this it was imperative to undertake a period of rest, as the energy hologram needed to heal and become cohesive in a new way.

Healing Hands

In this particular instance I was working with a small group of people. I felt my energies scanning one of them, and as this happened my hands opened up and energy flowed strongly towards one of the males in the group. My eyes focused on a dark spot far away in the distance (psychically). Immediately I sensed this dark spot was an energy representation of a deep-seated fear. Next I saw this man as a man of the cloth (priest/monk), and then heard the word 'Inquisition'. The next scene was not pleasant as it was a torture scene and I felt the intense fear that erupted within him. That was accompanied by an almighty wail of anguish and deep pain.

As this happened I felt the energy in my hands and arms continuing to intensify so that it became almost excruciatingly unbearable. The energy continued working on this man's hologram. I felt the energy seeking, going deeper and deeper within. Eventually it found what it was seeking – an energy remnant containing the embedded fear. The fear resisted as the energy emanating from my hands tugged and pulled even harder, eventually gaining hold and gradually pulling the memory (energy imprint) out and releasing it

The recipient of this release felt the whole intense experience. It was extremely uncomfortable for him during the actual process, though afterwards he felt immensely clearer and lighter within.

Physical Manifestation

In early 2006 I became aware of a small sore just above my right ankle. It was not infected and caused no discomfort. It was merely a small round sore, about ¼" in diameter. Some months later I noticed another similar sore on the left ankle. I was curious as to the cause of these sores and needless to say there was considerable speculation. For a while antibiotic cream was applied daily. However, it soon became apparent that applying cream to the sores was a waste of time as there was no change in their condition.

On an intuitive level I knew that there was no cause for concern. Eventually the reason for the puzzling sores revealed itself. One night I had a clear and lucid dream of another lifetime. The details were precise and sequential, and clearly demonstrated a time where I was betrayed by someone I trusted implicitly.

The sores on my legs had nothing to do with that particular lifetime. However, as the memory of betrayal surfaced, memories of other betrayals were also apparent. Obviously, there was a common theme of betrayal in my lifetime experiences and the energy of that memory was ready to be released. Once I had awareness that the sores on my legs related to a lifetime where I had been betrayed, placed in shackles and lost my freedom then the sores disappeared gradually.

The following is a clear and precise description of just how extensive and even painful an energy imprint can manifest. This description is taken from my book *A Square Peg: Conformity Isn't An Option* (written under pen name Gabriella Jaye). I'm including this because it demonstrates clearly the extent to which an energy imprint can impact the physical body.

An incident occurred just a few months after moving to New York State that was unnerving and even frightening. It presented a mystery and at the time there was no obvious outcome evident. Nine years later a greater comprehensive understanding of that particular incident finally occurred.

For a significant part of my life I'd experienced intense stomach pains. Visits to the doctor in earlier years resulted in tests and endoscopies being performed, which revealed absolutely no abnormalities. Apparently this was one of those cases where there was no physical indication of any illness condition despite consistent symptoms being present. Shortly after arriving in my new abode I awoke one morning with bleeding gums and blisters throughout my mouth. There had been no previous indication of anything wrong in terms of dental hygiene. There certainly hadn't been anything amiss the night before. Being intuitive I checked in with my body as to what was occurring. The mental conversation went along these lines:

"Do I need to go to the doctor?"
"No."
"Do I need to see a dentist?"
"No."
"Is what is happening in my mouth a physical condition?"
"No."
"Is it energetic?"
"Yes."
"Will it heal naturally?"
"Yes."
"What is happening? Why?"

There was no response to those last two questions. This obviously left only one possibility – to my mind anyway – that there was some energetic release process occurring even though it was manifesting as a physical condition. My relief was great. There was no option but to remain sequestered in my apartment as I didn't relish wandering out and about in the wider world with a mouth that looked hideous and might be considered contagious. My mouth definitely was not a pretty sight to behold.

Several days later, early in the morning I was in that in-between state of not being fully awake yet not still in deep sleep when suddenly a whole barrage of information flowed into my awareness. To this day I can still hear the information being clearly and loudly enunciated. The information stated firmly, "Your name was Lisette. You lived in Belgium during World War II and worked for the Resistance, and were the mistress of a German official. You were caught. Rather than betray the Resistance you swallowed a cyanide pill". While the wording of the message may not have been precisely as stated, this summary is exact in terms of the message content. Immediately I knew that the bloodied mouth blisters were cellular memory being released from that cyanide poisoning. I also intuitively had the awareness that the intense stomach pains experienced on and off during my adult years were also related or connected to this information.

Another important factor relating to this episode was that since childhood I'd experienced nightmares, all around the same theme. In the nightmares I was always in the woods or forests, hiding from soldiers and leading people away from the soldiers. Never in any recurring dream was I caught. However, the feeling of extreme danger was prevalent in the nightmare. As well, over the period of my adult years I'd been obsessively fascinated by any written material or films that detailed the atrocities that occurred and were perpetrated by the Germans during World War II. Watching the movie, *Schindler's List*, was a horrific experience. It unnerved me in inexplicable ways and I felt sick to my stomach at many of the scenes. As well, any stories relating to resistance fighters caught my immediate attention, and I had also gone through a stage of watching every possible DVD that dealt with stories about the Resistance fighters. Ironically, after receiving the information relating to the reason for the blistered and bloodied mouth two things happened. The nightmares ceased and my interest in learning more about resistance fighters and the Nazi treatment of them also came to an abrupt end. It felt as though I'd finally put to rest a memory that had plagued my subconscious for most of this life.

My understanding is that young children, generally up to the age of five years are most likely to have recall of other lifetimes. Usually after the age of approximately seven years children are fully immersed in their current life and any memories of other lifetimes have faded greatly. However, the painstaking work of psychiatrists Michael Newton, Brian Weiss MD and others indicates that memories can be brought to the surface during hypnosis regression sessions. There have also been countless reports of young children who are able to remember vividly details of other lifetimes.

Nearly ten years later I didn't anticipate the possibility of having any recall of Lisette's life in wartime Belgium. This particular story or memory remnant had been resolved, or so I thought. Regardless I was fully open to further exploration should there be anything else to uncover.

With this possibility in mind I again began reading books and viewing DVDs relating to German occupation during World War II. In particular my focus was on events and personalities involved in the underground resistance, as well as possible key German figures.

Being gifted with psychic abilities I sensed or felt that there might just be the likelihood of flashbacks and memories surfacing. I was open to all possibilities, and was fuelled by a determination to learn and understand as much as possible about Lisette's life, regardless of its possible brevity.

One instance where a memory was triggered occurred early on during the research period, which was undertaken during a long, wet and miserable winter. My partner at the time and I had commenced watching *Secret Army*, a BBC forty-two episode series, which depicted the Lifeline set up by an individual code named Yvette in Brussels and which managed to get a large number of pilots shot down by the German military back to England. This particular Lifeline was committed to only rescuing and returning airmen, and was not in any way involved in resistance, retaliatory or sabotage activities though at times the Lifeline workers interacted with different resistance groups. The *Secret Army* series, filmed in 1977 to 1979, was riveting viewing. There were numerous instances when I felt my body tense, clench in fear or react in subtle ways to the scenes. *Secret Army* was based on true life events, and some of the characters depicted in fact existed. As much as possible the series reflected actual incidents and personalities.

My partner was keen to explore further the possibility that Lisette may have been involved in the rescue and return of airmen to Britain. He used dowsing as a means of determining the validity of this possibility. Dowsing, when done correctly and with precision is a wonderful tool for determining truths and possibilities. It's a tool only, one that I've found to be reasonably reliable in providing accurate information. Anyhow, dowsing around the possibility of Lisette's involvement in the Lifeline came up negative. He commented, "I'm getting that Lisette wasn't involved with the Lifeline". My immediate and automatic response was, "She worked with the Communists in the Resistance. Her father was a staunch Communist so it became a family affair. Oh, and her uncle was also a Communist."

How in the world could I have known this? How reliable was this piece of information? Was there any way to verify it? Our conversation continued from there. By this stage I was in full flight, the words spilling out of my mouth of their own volition. "Communism in that time would now be viewed more as Socialism. The reason for the appeal of Communism was that its ideology was about equality, with everyone being equal, being viewed and receiving equally. The people were fed up with authorities, with the class system and with the elite being privileged while the rest of society was often denied basic rights." I went on in this vein for quite some time, very clear in my mind that the fervour of early Communism was the beginning of breaking away from the established class system.

Further research into the life of Lisette revealed that her real name was Marie-Louise Romu. She was born in July 1924 and died in Birkenau Concentration Camp in 1943. Her code name in the Resistance was Lisette. Possibly she may have been recruited by the French. She was directly involved in the sabotage of infrastructure, including the killing of Germans. Lisette was the mistress of a German Kommandant, possibly when in the concentration camp. She was betrayed by Belgium citizens, which led to her arrest. Lisette was initially sent to Auschwitz as a political prisoner and from there on to Birkenau. Her death was by cyanide poisoning, which was most likely self-administered in order to avoid interrogation.

The whole research process was evocative and filled with an intense mix of emotions. In my heart I felt that I was, or had been, Lisette. Would it be worth making extensive enquiries from authorities in Belgium? Did she have any family members still remaining that could be contacted? If so, would it even be possible to locate them and how would my story be received? Countless questions whirled through my head for weeks. There were two factors that I felt lent credibility to the possibility that I'd been Lisette in another lifetime. The first had been the physical manifestation of a cellular memory (energy imprint). I didn't imagine the bloodied mouth and blisters or the words that I'd heard clearly just before awakening all those years earlier. The second factor was that at different times I was able to explain things about life and conditions during World War II that consciously I'd had no knowledge of. The frisson of energy that would move along my body often was my intuitive way of saying "Yes, that's correct," whenever yet another piece of the puzzle was uncovered or solved.

During the time of undertaking this research there were many memories that surfaced, some extremely uncomfortable and painful. The research, however, finally put to rest the nightmare episodes, fascination or obsession with all things relating to the Resistance and the subconscious fear of authority figures.

Not all energy imprints are as intense as this. I'm sharing this particular experience so as to reassure you that in the world of energy, vibration and frequencies anything can happen. In fact, often when minor incidents and feelings coalesce they have the potential to actually support healing on deeper subconscious levels.

Symptoms of Energy Imprints

Over the years I have clairvoyantly seen imprints of swords, gunshot wounds, arrows, the blow of a solid instrument such as a wooden club, wounds inflicted by an animal or another person, fear due to a terrifying life experience, and more. There is no limit to the types of energy imprints contained within the energy hologram. If you can visualize any type of injury or fearful situation then there is a strong likelihood of an energy imprint manifesting.

It may seem that only destructive and negative energy imprints are stored as energy blockages or memories within the energy hologram. The reason for this is simple and straightforward. Loving, joyful and positive experiences do occur in life, and when they do their energy supports and heals the energy hologram into wellness and wellbeing. However, our civilization's history of brutality and conflict is well documented. The recurring theme throughout historical records is one of vengeance, battles, slaughter, survival in tough conditions, disappointment, harmfulness, and so on. The basest of human instincts and behaviour have been largely predominant in many lifetimes on Earth. It is for this reason alone that imprints remain embedded within the energy hologram.

To date I have become aware that energy imprints make their presence felt in various ways. Those listed below are by no means exhaustive. They are merely those I have encountered for myself and in my work with clients. Please note, when there is persistent pain or discomfort it is important to seek the help of someone who is able to diagnose whether there is an underlying medical condition requiring treatment.

1. An intermittent sense of discomfort or pain in a particular part of the body. Clients often comment that there has been mild pain in a specific area that has defied allopathic and natural therapies treatment. This manifestation of an energy imprint surfaces because it is ready to be released from the energy hologram.

2. An impending sense of danger or feeling unsafe. Often this is a fleeting, irrational response to a situation that may actually appear to be perfectly safe. An example of this is an irrational fear of authority figures. This reaction appears to be common to many people who have been persecuted for practicing magic, witchcraft and other supernatural phenomena in other lives.

3. Physical symptoms that appear to be a normal response to environmental situations. This includes unexplained rashes, welts, stomach pain, and other mild physical responses exhibited by the body. Often these may actually be an indication that the body is releasing stored emotion and/or memory.

4. Lucid dreams, especially when there is a recurring theme that is uncomfortable or distressing. This may be a means of alerting the conscious mind of stored memory that seeks healing.

It is common for individuals to store more than one energy imprint. Given that the human energy hologram is incredibly complex, storing information from all lifetimes, then it's also logical to expect energy imprints to become apparent at different times in your life.

A straightforward analogy of how energy imprints surface or make their presence felt can be explained in terms of tree logging. When an old tree is logged it is always interesting to read the age of the tree by looking at the markings or rings that are clearly visible inside the trunk. Trees that are a hundred or more years old have a large number of rings, with each ring encircling the previous marking.

Visualize the energy hologram, like the markings found on a tree trunk, as containing many layers, with each layer storing the memories and incidents of one or more lifetime. As healing occurs on the outer layer any stored energy imprints in that layer (and possibly in several other layers as well) is cleared. Assuming that healing is an ongoing process, there will come a time when another energy imprint makes its presence felt.

This is due to the fact that further layers are being, or have been released thereby revealing another embedded energy imprint. The presence of an energy imprint only occurs when it is ready to be cleared from the energy hologram.

Methods for Healing Imprints

Self-diagnosis of an energy imprint is not recommended. However, if you have been consistently experiencing any of the four symptoms listed above and have not been able to heal in spite of various diagnoses and prescribed treatments then it may be worth exploring the possibility of the existence of an energy imprint. Seeking the skills of an energy medicine practitioner may be worthwhile as a session may help clear the imprint easily with little or no anxiety or discomfort being experienced.

As well, there are a couple of straightforward techniques that can be adopted and which may provide improvement. Being energy sensitive, one way that I become aware of yet another energy imprint's presence is a gradual, nagging feeling that something is not quite right within my body. Usually it is located in a specific area and may feel as though there is an old wound, which produces a range of different bodily responses. These include tightness, itchiness, burning or the area feels out of balance. Please note that the suggestions below are shared because I've found them to be effective. There may be other appropriate methods available. I share what I know and have experienced and trust that you will figure out what works best for your needs and issues.

1. During quiet, reflective time – and this may be undertaken during meditation, - focus your mind on the area of discomfort. Feel the sensations that you experience coming from the area. Direct your mind to the area of discomfort and quietly ask, "What is this discomfort about?" You may not necessarily receive an answer, though you may receive a rapid insight or faint sense of something in particular. Irrespective of whether or not you receive an answer, give gratitude for the fact that this energy imprint has made its presence known. Then quietly affirm, "I bless and release this energy imprint with love".

It is not necessary to know the reason for the energy imprint. However, inquisitiveness is inherent within human nature and it is reassuring to know and possibly understand the reason for something occurring. If you do not receive an answer or insight, accept the situation. The information may be revealed to you at another time. Repeat this process numerous times, until you feel that the discordant energy is no longer present.

2. As with the previous strategy, it is important to be in a space of silence for this particular method of healing an energy imprint. Again, focus your mind to the area of discomfort and feel the sensations coming from the area. Take note of whether there is any emotional response elsewhere in your body. Next, bring your attention to your heart center. Feel the unconditional love stored within. Then, using your mind, gradually bring the energy from your heart center to the area where you feel the imprint is situated. Feel the heart centered energy totally surrounding the imprint. If you are unable to visualize this occurring then it is perfectly acceptable to imagine. There is no difference in the outcome - it is the intention that creates the situation.

   Now that the imprint is completely surrounded by healing energy from the heart center, visualize the healing energy slowly penetrating the imprint. As the penetration occurs visualize the imprint shrinking. Continue with this process until there is nothing left but healing energy in the area. The imprint has been healed with unconditional love. When ready you may choose to return the healing energy to the heart center or leave it there, as it has intelligence it will know when it needs to return.

   If you happen to discern an emotion elsewhere within your body that feels connected to the energy imprint then also move the heart centered energy to the area where the emotion is experienced. Similarly, envelop the emotion with the healing energy and continue doing so until the emotion feels healed.

3. In some instances the energy imprint requires persistence and time to be cleared and healed, especially if the imprint contains memory of numerous lifetime experiences and deep emotional issues. In those situations it is suggested that including both Steps

1 and 2 daily for as long as is necessary will facilitate healing more effectively.

Healing energy imprints involves learning about, and becoming sensitive to energy. Heeding the messages that the body continually gives out is another vital ingredient to understanding what is occurring.

As you become more intimately acquainted with the energetics of your particular energy hologram your intuition will guide you to greater understanding. At times the information you intuit regarding your energy hologram may seem weird or irrational. Do not dismiss as impossible anything that your intuition draws to your awareness. The more you learn to trust and accept the information that is transmitted in an almost imperceptible manner the stronger your intuitive abilities become. In time your skills in interpreting and understanding the symptoms as they appear in your body will become finely honed and you will be in a position of greater empowerment and responsibility for creating and maintaining your wellbeing.

In Chapter Six I focus on the modern medicine system and also on the power of the mind. Western medicine has both benefits and limitations and I'm including comments on it as I feel the subject of energy medicine (frequency and vibration) cannot be fully covered without acknowledging the role and function of western medicine in our culture. The power of the mind is another topic entirely and it is inherently connected with the concept of energy medicine and all that transpires within your energy hologram. Mind discernment and application will be discussed throughout several chapters as it is a potent and effective tool when used as originally intended, which is for creation and manifestation.

Chapter 5

Allow yourself the pleasure of exploring new opportunities. There are many pastures to experience. There are many games to enjoy. The pleasures of the human condition are heightened when you temper them with compassion and servitude. Childlike joyfulness in all that you do will become more prevalent. This characteristic is infectious and others will be inspired by this presence of mind and enthusiasm of life.

At times you may feel somewhat like a fish out of water: that is because you are choosing to live life in another reality. You are choosing to leave behind the drudgery, tediousness and fears of the shared reality many on your planet are choosing. It is all about choice. As you find yourself lightening within enable your energies to encompass those who are struggling to break free of the morass of the densities on Earth.

Lightly share your wisdom. Teach what you have learned. Teach so that others too may understand and experience a new reality, a reality that is unfiltered, one that does not come with distortion and lies. Though it may feel at times as if the journey is complex and uncertain, know that it is not. You are choosing to experience a range of situations and emotions. These are part of the human condition and enable you to better relate to people, issues and perceptions. That is all. All that you teach will manifest. All that you practice will bring forth results. Remain inspired. Allow yourself to be guided. Honour your creativity. (Channelled message via automatic writing, 2005)

Energy Parasites

My introduction to the concept, and even idea of, energy parasites occurred in the nineties. While I had heard about them I'd not given the topic any credence, mainly because it wasn't relevant to my life at that time. Hence it came as a complete surprise when I began experiencing emotional reactivity and extremes. Usually my moods are relatively balanced. I am not generally prone to fits of crying, exasperation and periods of what would be called depression or moodiness. However, as my emotions see-sawed and became more erratic my concern increased greatly. This was most definitely not me, nor was it my normal. I did not recognise this person or the erratic mood extremes. At some stage I mentioned my concerns to a colleague who suggested that possibly I had been possessed by an entity. That likelihood shocked me greatly. She recommended a trained shaman and after quiet and deliberate reflection I phoned and discussed what was occurring before actually scheduling an appointment.

Making the appointment was one of the hardest things I'd ever done. While I wished for whatever was creating this inner emotional chaos to be gone my thinking went along the lines of, "What if this doesn't work? What if the situation is exacerbated? What if I learn something horrible about myself that I'd rather now know?" As crazy as these thoughts seem now, at the time they were only a few of the countless mental ramblings and questions that poured through my mind during the period until the appointment time.

Upon turning up at the arranged time I was surprised to see three shaman practitioners waiting, all of whom were complete strangers. After a further explanation of what had been happening emotionally the shamans consulted with one another for some minutes. Then they worked on me for three incredibly long hours. The treatment involved a mix of various stages, which felt like torture and were excessively uncomfortable for the most part. Luckily the memory of exactly what occurred during the whole process is a blur. I remember being covered with ice at one stage. It was frigid and my shivering was intense. There were chants and incantations – to the best of my recollection. Toward the end of the three hours I was stood up, feeling both disoriented and uncertain, and my body was pulled and prodded. All the while there were further chants intoned. By this stage my mind was in a complete incoherent fog. Nothing made any sense to my rational self.

As this was happening I felt unfamiliar sharp and strong pains in my body, which eventually pooled into my lower back. Suddenly a force from deep within my sacrum pulled strongly outwards. At the same time my body was held in place by the shaman practitioners, who were gripping onto my arms with all their strength. Simultaneously an invisible energy force was expelled outward from the sacrum area. It came out with an immense and powerful whoosh. The pain of it was excruciating. I felt as though my body was being pulled, much like a bow when an arrow is about to be released. Afterwards my body crumpled in an ungainly heap, totally depleted. The entity, or energy parasite, had been exorcised. If ever I doubted the existence of energy parasites, or entities, that doubt was immediately extinguished. My body felt rubbery, I was hot and sweaty and unable to function coherently for some time after. This was not an experience I would ever wish upon anyone. Interestingly, those weary, teary, discombobulated emotions completely disappeared and to this day have not returned.

Many years later I found myself removing entities, or parasites, from clients. They can be referred to as parasites because that is what they actually are. They leach off an individual's energy, draining and impacting the individual's ability to function in a normal healthy manner. Sometimes it's just as easy to refer to the parasite as an 'entity'. In my experience the two terms are equally applicable and interchangeable. Below I share some situations that have occurred with clients as well as sharing the understanding that has arisen as a result of interacting with these less than desirable attachments.

Prior to an energy session a client experienced an extensive array of symptoms. This is her description of them. "I was lethargic and unmotivated. Not like depression, more so like being stuck. I felt like I was on the verge of getting sick all the time. I would often ask myself, "Am I sick?" My tummy hurt, little to no appetite, headaches, eye pain that was like a bruised feeling on the right, the left side had a bit of sandpaper feel under the lid. Nagging low back pain and hips ached. Unusual weight gain with visible cellulite. Disrupted sleep, and woke up feeling tired and achy. I'd often wash my face and try to pull away a web like, sticky feeling. I had increased body odor. I felt dark and dirty, no, muddy and didn't know why. I felt safest alone and isolated."

This client also recorded how she felt after the session. "I felt a bit woozy and disoriented like I do when traveling internationally. I needed to get my bearings. Drinking water helped, as did looking in the mirror. I thought the best thing for me would be to take an Epsom bath and snuggle with my puppy and sleep a bit. I noticed my eyes didn't hurt anymore and I had clearer vision, as if a haze had been cleaned off. I didn't realize my sight was unclear. The sky is the most obvious in clarity and colour as well as the trees, mostly outdoors it's clearer. Low back pain is dull. No headache. Light, relieved feeling as if I'd lost weight. No nausea. I let out deep sighs of gratitude throughout the day. I didn't talk much, very mellow and quiet. I felt different."

I have deliberately included this client's descriptions on how she felt prior to and after an energy session. While it may have appeared to be an energy healing session it was, in fact, far more complex. Without going into detail about the session it was immediately apparent that this client had energy parasite attachments. While this session was somewhat different to most energy work that I undertake, hers was not the first of these more challenging client appointments that involve clearing energy parasites or entities.

When this client arrived for her scheduled appointment I had no prior awareness of what was in store. In fact, she presented as well dressed, clearly articulate and highly intelligent. She appeared to be no different to the vast majority of my clients. It was only when she shared the multiplicity and range of symptoms that I immediately understood the reason for her visit. This client did not know or understand what was happening to her, she only knew that she was experiencing distressing and uncomfortable symptoms. These symptoms were relatively new and completely unfamiliar to her.

Before describing precisely what was occurring energetically in her energy hologram I will go back in time and share earlier understanding and experiences of a similar nature.

In my earlier book, *The New World of Self Healing*, I discuss the importance of protecting your energy hologram. Undertaking daily protection of your physical location and energy hologram is a powerful way of honouring the energy, frequency and vibration that you hold. As your hologram becomes clearer it holds more light, it becomes clearer and more radiant. When this happens you attract stronger energies, many of which will wish to attach to your energy in much the same way that a parasite finds a host body to support its life system. Parasite, according to the Oxford Dictionary means 'an organism living in or on another and benefiting at the expense of the other'.

When I psychically see an energy parasite I generally see a dark mass that has attached itself to the energy hologram of an unsuspecting person. Once attached this dark energy mass can create considerable discomfort, pain and stress for its host. Over time the dark energy expands and takes hold of a significant portion of an individual's energy hologram. In some ways it reminds me of garden vines that spread prolifically when left unchecked and eventually cover every possible portion of a host plant or tree.

Clearing an energy parasite requires skill and confidence, and possibly even an element of fearlessness. Fearlessness is not bravado. It's a surety in the ability to do the clearing, in understanding your strength and steadfastness in undertaking such a delicate and often complicated healing procedure. In religious organizations the clearing is often referred to as an exorcism. The demon energy to be exorcised is viewed as evil. According to the Church only someone with the protection of God can do this work. In shamanism there are rituals for specifically clearing negative energies (dark energy mass). Again, only someone who has been initiated as a shaman is considered skilled for this type of healing. In other words, anyone not initiated as a shaman or not working under the umbrella of the Church is considered unsuitable to undertake this kind of removal.

My non-physical teachers have instructed me on the process of clearing energy parasites, just as there are other energy medicine practitioners who are capable of undertaking such a clearing. At all times my protection is strong and there is no likelihood of an energy parasite leaving its host and attaching itself to my energy hologram. Needless to say, I have the utmost respect for these parasitic energies. They are tortured and have chosen to experience an existence of darkness. Sometimes they can be especially angry and volatile to deal with.

Some years ago a client came for a session and within a few minutes it became apparent that he was tormented spiritually. I found two parasites (or entities) trapped within his energy hologram. The first one was removed quite easily. The second, however, proved to be somewhat recalcitrant. It was located in his lower back and had extended a tentacle down his left leg and had inserted a hook into his left sole. My client was surprised at my description of what I saw, as he had recently experienced difficulty with his left leg, finding walking more of a challenge.

Another client's possession by an energy parasite was much more extensive and extreme. Initially I was shown (psychically) black tentacles throughout her energy hologram. These tentacles were deeply embedded in practically every part of her being. Unravelling the tentacles was a complex and lengthy process, lasting nearly ninety minutes. At the heart of the tentacles was an angry and hostile dark entity, whose reaction to the intrusive work was intense. It took every ounce of skill and confidence I had to complete the session. At the end of the session my client was exhausted, overwhelmed and confused. This particular parasite had existed within her energy hologram for too many years, probably for a large part of her life. It was literally like a garden vine that, over time, completely covers and chokes its tree host. After clearing this energy parasite my client felt disoriented for over a week. Some discernible aspects of her personality changed. She felt different and wasn't initially comfortable with her new, clearer self because it felt vastly different to anything she'd previously become accustomed to.

The client who kindly provided the two descriptions at the beginning of this chapter relating to her experience of energy healing was actually host to two energy parasites. In my experience it is unusual to find two energy parasites within one energy hologram. During the course of that particular session my client was interested in what could have caused her to attract the energy parasites. If you take the time to read her description of how she was feeling prior to the energy healing session you will discern some unusual symptoms, including feeling as though there was something sticky on her face. She also shared that she often contorted her face and found unusual sounds emanating from her throat. The two energy parasites were well established within her energy hologram. They most likely had been there for some, if not many, years and had become so dominant that they were in fact controlling aspects of her personality, moods and traits.

Possible Signs of Energy Parasites

Listing all possible signs of energy parasite possession has obvious limitations, as indications are often vague and may vary from person to person. The list below is not exhaustive and some of the indications may also relate to other indeterminate issues, including physical health conditions. If uncertain then, again, I highly recommend a visit to a medical practitioner to rule out any health issues.

- A sudden and highly unlikely change in general mood. Often clients tell me that they are generally positive and of a happy disposition when they unexpectedly begin to feel emotions of anger, hostility, resentment, and so on. Basically, a new set of mood behaviours that are uncharacteristic suddenly emerge. These moods are not in the least bit uplifting. They may also be suppressed emotions that can no longer be contained. Distinguishing between the two can be challenging. Usually erupting suppressed emotions run their course naturally whereas parasitic attachment slowly worsens over time.

- Pain in specific parts of the body that cannot be explained. Often the energy parasite lodges in the sacrum, sometimes in the solar plexus. Over time as the energy parasite expands there will be increasing pain in different parts of the body. A visit to a medical doctor may result, as a means of seeking explanation for the pain. Often, however, there may be no evidence of causative factors.

- Reduced energy. A parasite needs energy to thrive and its energy source is the light energy of its host. It should be noted that energy depletion could also be due to other factors that could possibly be rectified with diet, exercise, getting enough sleep, and other lifestyle factors.

- Contradictory thinking. Many clients report that their thinking processes undergo gradual change. Normal thinking patterns are reversed, with the client wondering what prompted their thinking. In other words erratic, uncontrollable thoughts become more normalized.

- Hearing voices that urge unconventional behaviour, possibly even putting the individual at risk of harm or danger.

- Unexpected and unusual changes in daily routines. This includes cravings for foods that normally would be shunned, a desire to smoke, consume more alcohol, indulge in substance and self-abuse, and to give up healthy activities.

When there is a marked deviation from normal behaviours and attitudes this may signal that an energy parasite has attached itself and is now asserting its basest nature upon an individual. In my client's case, described at the beginning of this chapter, she experienced some of the above signs. She also described herself as often battling with herself, particularly as she found herself being drawn to behaviours and attitudes that were not within her normal healthy repertoire and lifestyle.

Energy Parasite Attachment

Energy parasites are continually seeking a host body. Like most people on a path of self-awareness I became aware of these entities early in my days of seeking, especially when one attached itself to me. Its removal, as shared earlier, necessitated a three-hour session with three practicing shamans, and the force of its release was sufficiently strong to literally thrust my body more than a metre backwards.

When is an energy parasite likely to attach to a host body? What conditions are suitable or necessary for such an attachment to occur? Though I do not believe there is an exhaustive list of conditions or situations for energy parasite attachment, there are some instances when there is more likelihood of it occurring. These include:

- periods of intense and prolonged sadness and grief;
- on-going depression or lengthy periods of abject misery;
- using mind-altering substances;
- drinking alcohol to excess;
- having low self-esteem and perceiving life to be gloomy and miserable;
- engaging in paranormal experiences such as Ouija boards, poltergeist activities, etc;
- indulging in baser activities, including attendance at places where the energy vibration is of a lower frequency;

- feeling on-going emotions such as anger, judgment, resentment, hatred and so on, especially when these are the predominant emotions experienced;
- continually living a fear-based life; and
- having significant damage to the energy hologram, such as tears or rips, which cause weaknesses whereby an energy parasite can easily enter and settle.

It is likely that you will experience some of these conditions or situations at some stage in your life. When there is continuing focus or emphasis on any one or more of these then there is continuing weakening of the energy hologram. Often the energy hologram appears to be shattered, has holes or is imbalanced, which presents an ideal opportunity for an energy parasite to find and attach itself to a host.

Most individuals experience a mix of emotions and perceptions on a daily basis. When there are sufficient positive and strengthening energies continually being supplied to the energy hologram then there is less likelihood of an energy parasite attachment. Love, laughter, being part of a family and community, exercise, feeling passion for an interest and generally feeling good about life and about self are some of the traits that reduce and prevent the potential for parasite attachment.

Energy Protection

In the early days of my spiritual awakening I seriously questioned the need for protection of my energy hologram, believing that undertaking protection practice was a fear-based action. The energy of fear is potent and attracts whatever is feared! However, my non-physical teachers consistently urged me to undertake protection practice daily, which I diligently complied with. Contrary to this, many of my colleagues argued strongly that there was no need for protection practice. Their statement went along the lines of: "When you come from a position of love then that is all that is needed". One day, when I questioned my non-physical friends yet again they responded by asking this question, "You have a home?" to which I responded, "Yes". They then continued with, "Would you leave the doors and windows of your home open to all and sundry?" That was sufficient information for me to rethink my perspective, as I am discerning about who is invited into my physical and personal space. They then pointed out that choosing to not practice protection of my being was literally extending an open invitation to all energies, irrespective of frequency and vibration, to enter my energy hologram.

Their message was certainly clear and concise. Since that time I've also come to realize the truth spoken by those who maintained that love is all that is necessary. Most individuals hold pain and fear in their heart center and while that is the case I believe it's still important to undertake daily protection as a means of honouring your sacred energy hologram. If you are at a stage of awareness and know that your heart chakra and other chakras hold absolutely no fear, then it's unlikely there is any need for hologram protection to be undertaken. This is because the vibration of unconditional love is so powerful and when your energy hologram thrums with this frequency continually that love frequency actually provides shielding. It all comes down to perception and personal choice as to whether you choose, or not choose to undertake this practice.

One of the first things to recognize is the importance of not attaching any fear to the possibility of energy parasite attachment occurring. I emphatically stress this point. Energy parasites seem to possess a strong radar detection system when it comes to the energy of fear. When you fear something then the Law of Attraction instantly goes into operation. Once the fear reaches a certain intensity in strength then you will find you have attracted what is feared (or something similar).

There are numerous means of extending protection to your energy hologram. When this is done regularly, and preferably on a daily basis, then over a period of time strengthening occurs. It is perfectly acceptable to recite a short prayer seeking protection and safekeeping on a daily basis. Some people find a mantra that is appropriate to their needs. Others visualize a white bubble of protection that surrounds them. Often a lengthy protection ritual is established and this supports the process of ensuring an energy parasite free environment. While all these are effective the strongest protection of all is continually being in a state of unconditional love.

Realistically, maintaining unconditional love on a consistent basis can be challenging for most individuals, yet it is such a potent force and deterrent to energy parasites. Here I must provide a word of caution. It is normal to assert that love is all-powerful, that it is present and that you are pure, divine love. While these words specifically have some potency they also have definite limitation if they are merely thoughts and are not a true and constant state of being. Speaking words of love while still holding an element of unknown and unrecognized fear residing within affords insufficient protection. It is only when the heart center is open and a state of feeling love (instead of merely thinking and talking about it) is established that a natural all-encompassing love based protection becomes powerful.

Coming to a state of unconditional love involves the process of reiterating self-love and other heart centered love related mantras and affirmations. Giving gratitude many times daily provides a solid basis for the development of self-love and from there gradually building spiritual and energetic muscle, which ultimately manifests as a permanent state of unconditional love. Undertaking this practice supports the process of coming to a state of compassion and even bliss. Here I stress that it's a process. It may take longer for some individuals than others. Nevertheless it's a powerful motivation and goal that eventually has the potential to be life changing.

Proceed Cautiously

The reason I am writing about energy parasites is not to cause alarm or raise fears. Over the years I have encountered different types of energy parasites, of varying strength (power) and have seen the pain they have caused their hosts. This phenomenon is not widely written about, nor do many people easily understand it. I share my experience and understanding of this energy phenomenon so that you may have greater insight. And, if for some reason you believe that you may be experiencing an energy parasite I recommend that you contact a practicing shaman, religious authority qualified to assist you or an energy practitioner who has skills in releasing them from a host body. Under no circumstances attempt to do this yourself. This is definitely not a do-it-yourself activity!

However, if you feel that you may be hosting an energy parasite there are a number of things you can do to minimize its impact and to support your wellbeing. All these support the process of raising your energy frequency, thereby reducing the energy resonance that the parasitic entity craves. These include:

- praying and/or meditating daily, and in this state send love and healing to any energy attachments in your energy hologram;
- consciously focusing your thoughts and emotions in a positive manner. Every time you find negative thoughts and emotions surfacing immediately use your mind to cancel them and reframe into a positive and supportive statement or feeling;
- spending quality time with people of integrity and positive energies, as these will lift your mood and enhance the quality of your thoughts and actions;
- avoiding people and places that will lower your energy vibrations. If this is impossible then minimize, where possible, these contacts and always ensure that you place protection around your energy hologram;
- becoming diligent in ensuring that daily protection is practiced; and
- undertaking ancient tribal rituals such clearing your environment and energy hologram with smoke from a sage smudge stick, or using a sage protection spray.

One activity that can be undertaken in complete safety and will not require a great deal of time involves working with your energy to heal the darkness of the energy parasite. During meditation quietly focus your mind on the part of the body where you sense the energy parasite is located. With your mind focused quietly say, "I send you love. I send you light. I send you healing". Then bring your attention to your heart chakra and with your mind's eye visualize the energy from the heart chakra slowly moving to the area where the energy parasite resides. Next, slowly visualize (or imagine) the heart chakra energy fully surrounding and encapsulating the energy parasite. Feel the love surrounding and permeating the entity. Continue with this process for as long as you feel comfortable.

You may not be successful in clearing the energy parasite in one session. I suggest that you may need to repeat it again and again. However, there is a distinct advantage in undertaking this activity, as it may help reduce or limit its ability to grow within your energy hologram. In time it may even decide that the love energy you continually send is too strong and it may choose to leave your host body, or it may eventually even transmute into light!

Most importantly, if you choose to have the energy parasite removed then seek the skills of someone who has the expertise and knowledge to do this safely. As already mentioned, this is not a process to be attempted by an unskilled person.

Intention is Everything

After a lengthy period of stress, drama and unexpected changes in my life I felt, once again, that something had to give. It seemed that no matter whatever I did there were difficulties and challenges that appeared to be monumental and never ending. As I walked along the water's edge early one morning I again railed at my non-physical friends. My whines occurred from time to time, usually at a point where I'd reached the end of my patience. The complaints and difficulties poured out my mouth ceaselessly. It was a non-stop tirade, whine and rant.

I just couldn't believe that life could be this painful, and that the pain would be continuous. I asked, "Why?" Why was life so hard, so difficult? Why couldn't things just be easy for once? What had I done to attract such difficulties? Maybe I was having somewhat of a pity party but I needed to vent as I was fed up with the constant challenges. My perception was that surely after all the meditations, listening to sage advice from non-physical beings and also adhering to their guidance then surely it was time for my life to actually become a tad more comfortable and easy.

Once the rant was over I heard clearly, in my head, "How can you understand if you have not experienced?" That profound question stopped me in my tracks. In a fraction of a second I realized that everything happens for a reason, even when that reason is not apparent and that it may never become apparent. I also immediately had the awareness that my personal experiences would help me genuinely say, in empathy, "I understand" when clients shared their concerns. From that day my whining mostly stopped and my gratitude practice increased dramatically.

Rather than living in fear of attracting an energy parasite or of having an accident or of having something disastrous happening it's important to recognise and work with the power of energy whenever possible. It is energy that determines any and all outcomes. The bottom line is not what happens to you but how you view and deal with whatever occurs. Energy parasites love and thrive on the energy of misery and fear. Fear is a powerful human state. Yet it can be overcome and neutralized, as has already been shared.

Earlier I suggested using the energy of unconditional love from your heart center as an infusion. When used this way the heart centered energy imparts the vibration of love into every cell, atom and molecule in your body. While you may not see it happening I can assure you that it's a powerful technique. Merely placing the intention and visualizing it makes it real, according to the quantum sciences. The cells in your body respond to both the intention and any action that is undertaken.

Your response to feeling out of sorts and even possibly exhibiting some indications of an energy parasite is of primary importance. Should you feel gloomy and helpless that mood (energy/vibration) feeds whatever is sitting there. However, when you decide to shift your energy into a more positive state that in turn begins to minimise and even neutralise any potential for parasite growth and expansion.

If you have attracted an energy parasite then it's happened for a reason, as it did in my case. It is not the end of the world. Your situation can be changed providing you consult with a qualified person to help remove the parasitic energy. Whatever experience you may have with an unwelcome energy parasite it's unique to you, and is for your understanding relevant to your life situation. In time you will come to know its purpose. My personal experience has supported not only my learning and inner growth but also has generated a feeling of empowerment. This is my body. It's my responsibility to keep it functioning well and to ensure that it's not host to parasitic attachments. In my world my body is a sacred temple. I trust it's the same for you.

New Age Teachings

In recent years I've questioned the validity of a lot of the New Age spiritual information being espoused and shared widely. While this literature provides great insight and explanation on the meaning of life it often seems (to me) to provide a starry-eyed perspective on what being spiritual entails. This statement is not intended to be a criticism; it's simply my personal observation. While I strongly encourage and support individuals in their personal journey into greater consciousness and awareness I'm also cognizant of the fact that many people are unaware of the potential pitfalls along the way.

Activities undertaken to expand consciousness, to clear chakras, to reconnect with soul aspects, and more are all undeniably helpful in supporting an inner shift. I am the first to acknowledge this benefit. In fact, the proliferation of New Age materials and teachings has certainly helped heal deep seated wounds and provided great tools for creating and manifestation. This is a gift that the New Age teachings have provided for the masses.

My concern is that overall a rosy picture has been painted, one where love and light are all that exist. The art of discernment and caution are not readily espoused and encouraged. In fact, how often do you read about energy parasites, hooks, attachments and other such things that exist and which can create havoc and pain? It is not until you experience one or more of these that you begin to understand that discernment is critical to wellbeing and ongoing inner growth.

Not every entity or non-physical being that exists is love filled, nor does it come with higher consciousness and awareness. Nor do they necessarily end up becoming attached, as a parasitic entity, to your energy hologram. Often they may appear by your side as loving, supportive guides who encourage you and provide seemingly sage advice. From that initial contact a non-physical entity has the potential to guide you into a journey of uncertainty or chaos which may even result in some form of trauma.

What I'm attempting to emphasise is that any non-physical energy being has to earn your trust over a lengthy period. At the same time it's important that you continually apply discernment in your interactions. Does their energy feel consistently loving? Is the message and advice given in alignment with your innate goodness? Or does it in some way feel off? Do you feel discomfited or uncertain? In other words, what is your intuitive, gut feeling? If it feels consistently positive, supportive of your free will, lacking judgment and providing guidance then ultimately it's up to you as to whether you trust and accept what is being offered. You have free will. You have choice in these matters. It's okay to say no when something doesn't resonate or if you feel uncomfortable.

Often New Age teachings do not explain the downside of spiritual growth, nor outline the countless ways in which you may be challenged in your ongoing inner journey. Most individuals usually learn through experience, often without full understanding of meaning or ramifications. This in turn may result in a complete cessation of all inner searching, in the onset of deep fear or in the undertaking of a path that may result in unnecessary pain.

You would not put your hand on top of a hot stove; its heat as your hand nears the surface would warn you of potential risk. It is the same with interacting with non-physical entities. Go slowly, this is not a race. Take time to learn as much as is possible. Seek the wisdom of someone who has been a long time practitioner and who is able to support and guide you. At all times listen to your own intuitive knowing, your gut instincts, as they never lie.

There exists a dark side to the spiritual journey, in much the same way as Carl Jung proposed the theory of the Shadow Aspect in psychology. Understanding and accepting the dark side of self, and of the spiritual journey, ultimately provides self-empowerment to a degree that otherwise would not be attained.

As a final note to this sombre incursion into the realms of dark energy it's a worthy reminder that energy is simply energy. It has frequency, it has vibration. The New Age movement promulgates a message of love and light. Love and light cannot exist, or be evident, without the very opposite also being in existence. Dark energy can often be very powerful. Its power needs to be respected, and never taken lightly.

If, for some reason you have attracted an energy parasite or are being challenged by dark entities my repeated suggestion is to find a practitioner who is capable of supporting and helping you. There is always a reason for the experiences you attract. All experiences are for your growth and expansion into higher levels of consciousness, even when it doesn't always feel that way. I've learned that there is always someone with wisdom and insight to support you through these experiences. I've also learned to fully respect the dark energy entities/parasites and their power.

Through my own journey and experiences I've had plenty of

opportunity to study them, their tendencies and habits. Making a choice to simply ignore them wasn't an option. Instead, through a process of study and practical undertaking it became obvious that the kindest action was always to be in a space of unconditional love towards them as this is the most potent force that limits and minimizes the likelihood of attachment. The final and most powerful technique is to undertake regular protection/ shielding of your energy hologram. This is an act of self-love, self-worth and self-empowerment.

Chapter 6

Tuesday I had my first acupuncture session. It was transforming. The session took 90 minutes. My whole history was explored then assessment took place. This was Chinese diagnostic assessment. Seems that my heart is lacking **joie de vivre,** *not surprising given that the monotony and boredom of the days are beginning to get to me! As well, my spleen is not in a happy place (spleen means not being sincere with yourself and others by not loving yourself or others, or both). As well there were blockages in the gall bladder (you are letting something stop your beingness), stomach (you are not taking the time to understand the things you do, so you can grow to feel positive), digestive system and liver (you are not learning about why you allow others to hurt your feelings). Basically most of these are about not loving myself fully, about non-acceptance and judgment. I feel that these relate to experiences earlier in this lifetime and in other lives – and are not necessarily relevant to the present life situation. However the release of these emotions is essential for healing to occur.*

Surprisingly, my health is actually very good, with chi flow being strong and vital. The twenty minutes of having numerous needles placed strategically in my back was pure bliss. Afterwards I felt totally re-energized and alert. That feeling remained until around the middle of the night. Then the pain commenced. The energy in my legs pulsated and throbbed. My stomach and spleen felt as though they were suffering from pins and needles. There were a myriad of sensations, many of them uncomfortable, working their way through my body. Feel there was a major realignment of energies. Since then my legs have loosened considerably. My energy levels have increased dramatically and general feeling of wellbeing is positive! A massive change all over. (Journal entry, 2005)

Western Medicine

During the course of his life Albert Einstein is attributed with having made many insightful and profound statements about the nature of life, reality and the cosmos. His incredible wisdom and knowledge have added a richness of understanding to our lives. Einstein was truly a man before his time. One of his statements that fully resonates is: "Future medicine will be the medicine of frequencies." My understanding of the frequencies has been taught by those non-physical beings that have been my companions and teachers over many years. It is for this reason that I'm actually devoting a part of this chapter to the exploration and discussion of western medicine, mainly because western medicine is not about energy and frequencies. Maybe one of these days there will be changes in perspective and understanding of the interconnectedness between physical and energetic levels, which will bring about reform to the system.

How you react or how you view the model of medicine that's been forced upon an unsuspecting population is up to you. Your reality and perception may be totally different to mine and is valid for you. That is something I fully understand and respect. However, I trust that you will read my analysis of western medicine with an open mind. My intention is to expose the disparity between energy medicine (frequencies) and the model currently controlling the health system. Hopefully you will come to understand the limitations of the western medicine model and allow your capacity for questioning to look deeper into the nature of the physical body and its interdependent relationship with the energy hologram.

As you will come to realize I am not a fan of western (allopathic) medicine for a variety of reasons, though I acknowledge that no one size fits all. By this I mean that allopathic medicine is an option or choice that works for some individuals, though not necessarily for everyone. I feel it beneficial to share what I feel are its limitations and the reasons for that understanding. Straight off I will happily say that if I were involved in a vehicular accident, injured in another way or was facing a serious health or medical condition I would not hesitate to seek out allopathic treatment and services. Having gotten that admission off my chest I will clarify that statement with a proviso. The proviso being that my first and foremost thoughts and action would be to explore natural therapies and energy medicine treatments to support and promote healing. This perspective is mine because I know its benefits and innately prefer natural therapies for my personal health and wellbeing.

The history of allopathic medicine has greatly compartmentalized a particular subject of study, that is the human body and its functioning. Consequently it appears that a holistic approach has gradually vanished from the practice of western medicine. It's commonplace to have medical staff specializing in limited and specific fields of study. A cardiologist deals with heart related issues. A nephrologist works with patients going through the process of renal failure. An oncologist specializes in cancer. I'm sure you're beginning to get the picture. Sadly these particular fields of study do not overlap. They are pigeonholed and separate from one another. Thus an allopathic medical practitioner is legally required to provide a service in their field of specialization only.

All the while there's massive funding and research undertaken in each of these dedicated medical fields in order to understand the microscopic nuances of human biology and the nature of disease. Research involves experimentation, as it always has done. If you are familiar with medical history you'll know that a great deal of what is known and understood about the human body is thanks to the dissection of human cadavers. Grave robbers were prolific in finding cadavers for medical research in the nineteenth century. Body snatching, a common practice two hundred years ago, was a gruesome practice but it revolutionized the understanding of how the body works and the damaging impact of disease and illness.

From this practice doctors at the time learned how organs function, how they become ravaged by disease, what happens with ageing and also how to better understand the intricate functioning of the human physiology. In particular, it enabled doctors to significantly improve amputation techniques. Despite this tough beginning there's no doubt that grave robbers provided a massive service to medicine. Without their risky business it's unlikely there would be such intricate understanding of the physical complexities of the human body or that microsurgery and organ transplants would ever have evolved to the highly sophisticated level that are now commonplace.

Limitations

Where do I begin to explain my perceptions around the shortcomings of allopathic medicine? As a non-medical person my familiarity with the terminology is limited. My awareness of the core issues is most likely extremely narrow. Yet I've studied both physiology and anatomy and have always been fascinated by the intricate complexities of the human body and how it functions. Malfunction and illness intrigue me, as I attempt to make sense of the reasons behind whatever may be happening. In my years of working with the energy hologram (energy medicine) my interest in the whole body – its foibles, inherent weaknesses, reasons for illness or optimal health, ability to heal or not heal have all held a fascination. It is this inherent interest in health and wellness that began nearly fifty years ago that guides my knowledge and concerns about the limitations of allopathic medicine and also of the drawbacks in relying on it solely for health and wellness concerns.

My reservations are listed in no particular order of importance or merit. There may be other areas of concern or others not identified which may benefit from further discussion. Nevertheless these reservations are merely a way of expressing my disquiet. You as the reader may agree or disagree. I encourage you to question, analyze and also reflect deeply on whatever is shared. Your perceptions and beliefs are equally valid. All I suggest is that you deeply question your beliefs and understanding and what guides them. Explore how they were accepted into your belief structure and why you may hold some certain positions more strongly than others.

My journey has involved significant research and questioning. It has been an ongoing process for a significant portion of my life. A great deal of my reading has been of scientific and medical research reporting. During the course of my life I've seen numerous medical facts disproved. I've seen medicines touted as being a wonder drug only eventually to learn that they have proved to be ineffective or dangerous. The limitations discussed below are merely observations based on nearly fifty years' interest in matters pertaining to health and wellness. As an energy medicine practitioner my focus and emphasis is always on prevention and restoration of the energy hologram into a state of balance, as this then supports the process of healing on the physical level.

1. The study of western allopathic medicine is compartmentalized, which means that the body is not viewed or treated as a whole energetic entity. My intuitive understanding is that every body system and function is interconnected with practically everything else that exists within the whole hologram structure. For example a cardiologist specializes with heart functioning. Surgery and medication are the common ways of relieving blockages or other issues that impede strong heart health. A cardiologist does not treat nutritional deficiencies, or venal problems that may arise or may contribute to heart disease. Nor is the cardiologist qualified to provide a recovery and fitness regimen needed for full recovery. Thus an individual having experienced a heart health issue requires the specialized skills and treatment of possibly three or four other specialists. In addition, it's generally physical factors only that determine treatment. Emotional components are overlooked or may even be deemed unnecessary Yet, is it possible to die from a broken heart? Is it possible for a lifetime's accumulation of relationship rejection to weaken the heart muscles? To what extent could emotional and mental stress be a pivotal contributing factor?

2. It relies heavily on surgery and medications (drugs). It is common for individuals as they age to be prescribed drugs for a condition that may or may not be life threatening. All drugs have side-effects, and reactions to a prescription may then result in another prescription being given to overcome the side effects. And so on it continues until a veritable cocktail of chemical drugs change the chemical, electrical and neurological functioning of the body – both physical and energetic. In addition, some drugs are well known to cause side effects to organs and body systems. Yet how often do you hear the recommendation for healing being simply fresh air, exercise, eating nutritious meals, spending time in nature, meditation or learning de-stress techniques? In other words, the remedies of old, which were once the standard prescription of the family doctor, seem to be long discarded and forgotten.

3. Symptoms, however vague and unable to be diagnosed tend to be treated in many instances with exploratory surgery and/or medications that may or may not help. This generally results in the

individual becoming a guinea pig for pharmaceutical products as the allopathic medical system looks solely to their treatment as a possible benefit. Instead, in some instances there may be another explanation and another possible healing outcome without any long-term drug impact. Energy medicine recognizes the subtle effect of various factors including sub-conscious memory, fears and emotional trauma in contributing to illness or health related issues.

4. Allopathic medicine ranks high on cause of death, after heart disease and cancer. These are broadly labelled Iatrogenic Causes (medically induced) and it's difficult to determine the exact number of medically induced deaths per year due to surgery, prescriptions and other medical causes as often they are not reported as such. According to Australian Government figures (aihw.gov.au) there were over 26,000 potentially avoidable deaths in 2016. In the States it's the third highest cause of death and in 2003 research figures indicated that 225,000 deaths occur annually due to unnecessary surgery, medication errors, miscellaneous errors in hospitals, infections in hospitals and negative effects of drugs. It was also suggested that this figure was somewhat conservative, with some speculation that the number might possibly be much higher. I ask the question: How many deaths result from energy (frequencies) medicine and/or natural therapy treatments?

5. Another concern about allopathic medicine is the fact that there is an unwillingness to recognize the value of other fields of study including homeopathy, acupuncture, chiropractic, essential oils – all of which have a long history of efficacy and success rate in countries worldwide. Germany led the field of research in homeopathy, which has been practiced for generations. The Chinese medical system has demonstrated the high level of success acupuncture and the use of traditional Chinese herbs have achieved in many areas of health over thousands of years. These are only two areas out of many that have been vilified and deemed unmedical by those controlling the western medical system. I personally have seen the power of energy medicine in healing many conditions, often in instances where allopathic medicine

has been tried and has failed. In most instances, energy medicine and other natural therapy modalities are seen to be the last option or hope for individuals.

6. Finally, I see little, if any, integration of the Body, Mind and Spirit concept in allopathic medicine. Personally I prefer to think of it as being body, mind and soul, the reasons for which will be explored later. How is it possible to separate the body's functioning from that of the mind/intellect, the emotions or soul? How is it possible to ignore the powerful instincts that drive people into action? Or, what role does upbringing, beliefs, programming and transgenerational patterning contribute to illness? How does deep emotional trauma or stress trigger illness conditions? What does continual, habitual worry, which I call 'mental gymnastics' eventually create in the body? Ignoring or overlooking the non-physical factors and focusing solely on the physical manifestations of illness or injury I view as the biggest flaw embedded in the allopathic medicine model. From my perspective it's an incomplete model because it's fragmented and deals solely with only one level of functioning – the physical body.

It has to be obvious that our western way of dealing with health issues is not effective. I could go on about the increasing numbers of new illnesses, escalating health costs and the rising expense of health insurance. Ill health has become an acceptable state of being for a significant portion of the population in western culture. Realistically it can be said that real and lasting healing is not being achieved because attention is not focused in the right direction or on all possible directions. Scientific research and developments deal with the physiological and anatomical aspects and is generally limited to facilitating healing of the physical body. The figures mentioned previously, demonstrating the high rate of iatrogenic deaths are an indication that this methodology isn't achieving promising results.

While it's not my intention to labour the point regarding some aspects of allopathic medicine, I'm drawing attention to it because I've heard countless stories about the inadequacies of this system. It operates diametrically opposite to all that I've learned about the energy hologram and its functioning. Nevertheless, like all systems it has its strengths and weaknesses. Realistically all systems benefit from regular, thorough examination and analysis in order to pinpoint areas that need improving and modifying. Having had a lifelong interest in health matters it appears to me that health has become a business, a highly profitable and regulated business. Early medicine certainly did not start off in this manner. Its focus was on care and healing for those in need, and was not about budgets and profits!

The metaphysical approach, dealing with emotional, spiritual and mental states in a holistic manner is a healing methodology that is gaining acceptance and is often used in conjunction with standard allopathic medical treatments, where the patient deems it necessary. In many instances it's actually the preferred treatment for people worldwide. The metaphysical approach is holistic; it treats all the levels discussed previously in Chapter Two. The relationship between emotions and physical pain is explored and treated without western medications. Instead, an all-inclusive approach is applied. This means that a comprehensive history of an individual is taken prior to a determination of the best method of treatment. Basically treatment is tailored to the needs of the individual rather than merely a medication or treatment being prescribed.

Information provided by non-physical beings via channelling has referred to the limitations and even dangers of the allopathic medical system, in addition to issues of lifestyle being damaging. A channelling around the turn of the century states:

> "Whenever your body absorbs drugs, whether licit or illicit, there is a deleterious impact or effect on your energy grid system (hologram). Whenever your body undergoes medical surgery or exploratory treatment, again the energy system being highly sensitive, experiences misalignment. Your body is also affected by lifestyle factors including cigarettes, stress, suppressed emotions, negative thoughts and actions. In other words, anything that is not of a loving, supportive and positive energy. So, whenever it is that you come into contact with any of these, whether it be surgery, drugs, toxins, stress, chemical reactions, your body reacts accordingly. By this we mean there is

misalignment of energies resulting in a lack of balance and consequently a feeling of ill health or unwellness.......
In your modern medicine you have come up with very plausible explanations about the physical reasons for the appearance of symptoms, and so treatment generally is given for a specific condition. Often that treatment is a prescription for further medication, which in turn further upsets the finely balanced structure of your energy system."

People are unique. Each person possesses a unique biochemistry. One size does not fit all, especially when it comes to health and wellbeing. This is despite the marketing of pharmaceuticals that do their best to convince the public that it's as easy as taking a pill. It's not. A pill does not cure; it may reduce the symptoms just as much as it may create unwanted side effects.

The Mind

"As you think, so it is." I do not recollect where I first heard this simple though powerful quote. I've since become aware that it's been repeated numerous times in a similar format and with the same intention and meaning. In recent times Dr Wayne D Dyer is credited with saying something similar. His statement was: "Keep reminding yourself; I get what I think about, whether I want it or not". So, what does it mean? What is its relevance to health, wellness, spirituality and energy medicine? The reason for using the term "energy medicine" is that it is a form of medicine, not as a physical substance that can be ingested or inhaled, but more as an overarching umbrella that encompasses numerous holistic modalities that all work as a healing potency on some level within the human energy hologram. I deliberately call it medicine because it has a healing benefit that's been demonstrated countless times worldwide.

The mind is an incredibly powerful tool. It creates or manifests illness just as it has the potential and capability to create healing. Its power will be unravelled and explained further throughout some of the following chapters. When used constructively the mind is an incredibly potent means for creating change and manifesting untold opportunities for enhanced wellness, awareness and increased growth in consciousness.

Unfortunately in our current reality there's been extensive subliminal brainwashing, which has steadily increased the belief that mental (mind) health is a disease, is perfectly normal and can be medicated. The medical association between mind and mental health does little to enhance the actual truth about the magnificent ability of the mind. Instead, the mind is viewed as something that has to be controlled and that there has to be a sameness in how individuals view and experience reality. This is, I believe, a tragedy that's been perpetrated on an unsuspecting public. The fact that mental health has become what may be perceived as a national crisis is disturbing, to say the very least, especially when the true potential of the mind to create and manifest is being obscured and even ignored.

The field of psychiatry has had a significant role to play in defining mental health. The list of mental health disorders listed in the Diagnostic and Statistical Manual of Mental Disorders (DSM) is beyond belief, as are the countless medications recommended for such mental health issues. The current issue, DSM-5 contains over 1500 pages and is definitely a hefty volume. If you doubt the veracity of my comments I highly recommend you read *The Mind Game*, by Phillip Day, investigative reporter. His comprehensive tome outlines in great detail the history of psychiatry, the development of its legitimacy as a medical profession as well as the purpose and dangers inherent in this particular field of medicine. Day's investigation is not the only analysis that's been undertaken on the field of mental health. While it's not my intention to disparage all forms of mental health or the care of individuals who are subject to mental health issues I am concerned that it's become all too easy to define anyone who thinks outside the normally accepted parameters of societal norms as having a mental health disorder. My concern is that it's possible for normalization to be imposed, and subjugation of creative thinking to occur due to the influence of a medical field of operation.

As a young child I heard voices, lots of them, as is often the case with young children who are more susceptible and sensitive to the non-physical realities. Like many young children I also learned that this was not acceptable to my family due to their fear of my being mentally ill or being less than normal. At a later stage in life those voices reappeared, for which I'm deeply grateful, as they've been my guidance, my support and my trustworthy confidantes.

It is not unusual to hear voices, to see non-physical things and to also know or foresee that which is still to happen. In fact, it's far more normal than the average person would suspect. Over the years I've had countless friends, colleagues and clients share their paranormal experiences. The common consensus has been that these stories and experiences cannot be shared with their respective families and friends. To do so opens an individual to ridicule, disparagement and possible diagnosis of a mental health condition.

There is no doubt that instances of schizophrenia, bi-polar and other conditions impact individuals negatively, thereby creating chaos and uncertainty in their lives. As yet, however, our medical system has not been able to delineate between positive non-physical mind experiences and negative mind experiences. This, hopefully, in time will be explored and greater understanding and acceptance developed.

Discussing mind and mental health is a contentious issue. I'm not an expert on diagnoses and treatment of mental health issues, something I leave to professionals in the field. Instead I'm adept at reading the subtle energies and understand the role they play in your everyday life. In reading the energies I often see the energies in the layer of the mental body as being chaotic and disjointed. In much the same way I sense or feel the energies in the emotional layer as being filled with grief, anger, pain, resentment and so on. Each layer of the human energy hologram has distinct characteristics and functions, which are readily evident to the sensitive practitioner.

Differentiating between the mental body and the mind is another challenge. Is the mind in the mental body? Are the two one and the same thing? Or are they different? Where does the role of the brain come into the equation? All these are valid questions. In particular, there's been a significant amount of research into exploring what the mind is and where it is located. It seems, if my understanding of all that I've read, that the mind does not sit within the brain, though the brain processes and filters information. The mind apparently exists throughout the physical and non-physical aspects of the body - the energy hologram. This means, I assume, that cells transmit, receive and process information on the subatomic level. If that's the case then the human body in all its physical and non-physical aspects could possibly even be said to function or operate as a massive computing system. This possibility further supports the contention that the energy hologram is essential for survival. It could even be argued that without the hologram (or super computer) the physical body could not survive or even thrive.

Powerful Tool

As stated previously, the mind is a powerful tool for creating and manifesting. This particular fact cannot ever be underestimated or ignored. Hence, I stress this fact frequently because it is so important to maintain a state of mindfulness. Because of its powerful capability, the mind is able to create both magnificence and chaos in daily life. Thoughts create whatever is experienced. Here you may differ on that perspective but hopefully as you read the following chapters you will come to understand exactly what is meant by these statements. You may question the role emotions play in reality creation. They actually have a pivotal role. Yet an emotional response or feeling is triggered by a thought, often in memory or subconscious form, but a thought nevertheless is the trigger for an emotional response.

It is my intention in the following chapters to include information, suggestions, ideas and strategies for refining and honing your thought capacity (mind) to support your journey into greater awareness, healing and consciousness. Using the mind for creation is not just about developing interesting hobbies or advancing strategies for solving issues or problems. Such mind power is somewhat banal and could possibly be labelled 'lateral or creative thinking'.

Realistically the mind continually creates, even when thoughts are random and erratic. The results from such thinking processes become evident in a chaotic and even conflicted life. It becomes a mix of the good, bad and the indifferent. Whatever is experienced in life is a by-product or consequence of thought from both the conscious and subconscious minds. It is not my intention to labour the point on this, merely to draw your awareness and attention to the power of the mind, via the thought processes. In understanding this, it then becomes easier to refine your thought patterns, to reduce mindless chatter, to monitor and become mindful of the energy vibration your thoughts hold and create. This is important in working with your energy hologram. It is ideal to support alignment and consistency in all levels of energy functioning. This in turn creates a stronger, healthier and more powerful energy hologram. It also supports the shift into higher frequencies of consciousness.

The power of the super-conscious is generally overlooked and undervalued in reality creation and manifestation intention. I am not a fan of the word 'super-conscious' as it sounds rather clinical or Freudian. Instead I prefer to personalize it. A term that I find is easily accepted and understood instead is 'soul'. Hence you will find references to 'soul' and 'voice of the soul' scattered throughout the following pages.

Using the mind consciously and intentionally in the initial stages is an important phase in healing the body of old cellular and energetic memories. This process supports a shift in energy frequency. Over a period of time the shift to working with the soul becomes evident. It's a subtle shift, one that ultimately will enable you to know and understand yourself in new ways. During this process of working with your energy hologram you will peel away the layers of stagnant energy slowly and steadily. In the process erroneous beliefs, patterning and programming will be released until you eventually discover deep within that precious gemstone that is the real you. This is the process I referred to in the Introduction. This is the process of releasing limitations that keep you feeling stuck and which hold you in patterns of emotional reactivity and old pain memories or which prevent you from reaching your higher potential.

As you are no doubt beginning to realize there's a great deal of complexity and many concepts and layers to work with when you make the decision to actually go deeper and figure out how to become unstuck. Becoming authentic means peeling away the limitations and resistances held deep within. Living fully with integrity becomes a reality once the essence of who you really are is finally revealed. This is when the voice of your soul, the intelligent consciousness that is you is able to live in alignment with your purpose or mission, enabling fulfilment and joy to be permanent companions in everyday life.

The manner in which I write makes everything sound simple and straightforward. It's being shared this way because it is simple. Life is not meant to be overly complicated. Nevertheless, as I mentioned in the

Introduction the teaching I was privy to was shared in a simplistic manner in order to make it understandable. The actual science of quantum energy and consciousness is far more convoluted and complex. It is through gleaning some of the basics of energy and how it works that you have the potential to shift your frequency to a level that supports your spiritual evolvement, without mental dogma or limitations.

If you are wondering how best to move your focus constructively between mind, emotions and hologram functioning I stress that they are not separate entities or energies. However, there are steps that can be undertaken to support greater ease of functioning and flow between those particular areas. If there's one thing I've learned from clients it's that humans have a tendency to overthink, to constantly question and to engage in those never ending mental gymnastics. Next I explore the potential for reducing greatly the mental exhaustion induced by constant ego questioning and analysis. I encourage you to seriously undergo the following practice to support your endeavours to connect fully with your highest wishes and potential.

Emptying the Mind

Practices that reduce the constant mental merry-go-round of mindless chatter include meditation, tai chi, qi gong, breath work and other martial arts techniques. For many years I undertook regular meditation practice and certainly felt its benefits. However, it was not until the energy of the soul that incarnated as Edgar Cayce merged with mine for over four years that I learned a much more powerful technique. I had the good fortune to connect with the energy of this wise soul and to be the recipient of his non-stop teaching and urgings. The powerful and relevant information channelled through me was later published in *Edgar Speaks: Inner Transformation, 2012 and Beyond and Earth Changes*. In addition to channelling I was privileged to have his voice communicate with me on an almost daily basis. His voice would start yammering in my ear at night as my body was relaxed and preparing for sleep. It was during this time that his personal tuition provided the support I needed in terms of my own understanding and development.

At that time I'd erroneously believed that I was fully living in the moment. There's no doubt that humans are masters of delusion! Living in the moment I'd believed was gained through simply saying "I'm living in the moment" at every opportunity and then supporting that with twice daily meditations. How wrong I was. Nothing could have been further from the truth of the matter. Edgar's voice prompted me to use breath as a means of moving fully into the moment. This was the process needed to fully become one with the mind. By first reducing and then eliminating thought (ego mind) the voice of the soul (the true mind) was then able to be heard when it spoke.

It started simply and was actually far more difficult than I'd imagined. In fact, it took about three years' constant practice to actually achieve some consistent level of competency and mastery. Nevertheless, like every journey there had to be a starting point and I realized over time that the breath work made such a difference, one that regular meditation had never quite achieved. My experience of shifting from meditation to breath work is not unique. I've heard firsthand how others have enjoyed similar benefits.

The process I followed is very simple, yet not easy, and as I share this I encourage you to find your own way or style of shifting from mental gymnastics to a state of non-thought, thereby being in a space of fully utilising the mind for creating and manifestation. I use the word "non-thought" to describe this wonderful state, a state where the mind is completely free of thought and where an induced state of feeling stress free exists.

The first stage of this practice was to mentally say "Inhale" on the breath inhalation, "Circulate" on feeling the breath circulating throughout the body and "Exhale" on the breath exhalation. When mentally saying the process of inhalation, circulation and exhalation you will find that there's no room for thought. In addition, your awareness is drawn to the breath and its movement throughout your body. Initially I practiced this simple exercise for two minutes and then gradually increased it up to five minutes at a time, several times during the day. Two and five minute time limits can seem never ending when mentally saying, "Inhale, circulate, exhale" over and over again.

The first obvious sign of something different happening was that those pesky conscious and subconscious thoughts were unable to intrude when focus was fully on the breath. The second sign was a feeling of complete relaxation and de-stressing in the body. This indicated, to me anyway, that constant thinking results in feelings of stress throughout the body. After months of daily intermittent practice I felt the need to test my ability to stretch beyond the five minute period of deep breath work. I was due in Woodstock, New York, for an afternoon's work with clients. The drive normally took up to sixty minutes, and along the way I needed to stop at a tollway and pay a fee. My intention was to focus on the breath the whole way and to be in that profound space of non-thought.

Needless to say there was a considerable amount of mental self-talk prior to leaving home. "Remember to observe without mentally adding comments or judgments. Focus only on what is occurring in the moment. Observe it and then let it go." This I felt would be the best way to maintain a state of non-thought. With this intention I prepared for the trip, placing the money required for the road toll within easy reach. Taking several deep breaths to help empty my mind I began my challenge. The drive to Woodstock was effortless. I was fully aware and appreciative of my surroundings without attaching any thoughts to the large billboards or sights along the way. The journey felt endless, seemingly taking forever. There were no thoughts to distract my attention as I was able to fully focus on the breath. It was also unusually relaxing. Upon arrival at my destination I discovered the drive had been about ten minutes shorter in duration than usual, without having exceeded the speed limit at all.

Other observations made about the power of non-thought are the result of personal experience, and often occurred when driving. For example, focusing on the breath allows deeper calm and relaxation while also supporting heightened alertness when driving. I learned that traffic lights would most often be green, even when going through a series of traffic lights. Yet as soon as thoughts entered my mind the traffic lights would go red. In a state of non-thought there was also greater ease and flow of traffic. Once thoughts percolated through then other drivers would unexpectedly change lanes, brake suddenly or there were other sudden interferences to the traffic flow.

Harnessing the power of the mind begins with stilling the mind, emptying it of random thoughts. The benefits of using focused breath work are that it is undertaken with both eyes wide open and can be undertaken continually in everyday situations. Both the right and left hemispheres are engaged in the process, whereas meditation is a right brain activity. As well, it is possible with regular breath work practice to engage in conversation and other normal daily activities while being in a non-thought state. In fact, the ideal is to become adept at focused breathing so that you are largely in a state of non-thought for most of the day's activities. Of course, there are exceptions when you are required to think, analyse and problem solve.

In order to fully explore and master the power of the mind it is important to develop your skills of non-thought. The state of non-thought is where your ability lies in order to tap into your higher consciousness and to fully become the powerful manifestor that you truly are. The power of the mind in working with your energy hologram will be further explored in later chapters. However I encourage you to commence the focused breathing technique described above. As you begin to develop strength with it and progress along you will notice that the need to mentally say, "Inhale, circulate, exhale" will no longer be necessary. The process will become automatic once you focus on it, and this focus is attained by steadying yourself, emptying your mind and commencing the breath work.

As I mentioned earlier, it took me three years of consistent application to develop consistency and competency in being in a state of non-thought. The benefits were ongoing and surprising. At times I became frustrated with myself. Yet, once the benefits coalesced into a powerful and healthier mindfulness of existence I knew that there had been a massive shift within my consciousness. It was well worth the persistence, and for that I'm deeply grateful to the energy of the soul that embodied as Edgar Cayce. I learned a great deal about myself during this process, invaluable understanding that with a clear non-thought mind anything is possible.

Chapter 7

It was not until I finished working with my second client that it became apparent my thinking faculties were impeded. My third and final client for the day asked a question about my phone number. I couldn't remember the number! There wasn't time to focus on what seemed to be a momentary lapse in memory, though it was most unusual as I have a great facility for remembering numerical sequences. While working with this particular client I suddenly began to move rapidly in and out of multiple realities simultaneously. The experience was both unsettling and uncontrollable. With every breath I found myself moving through one reality to the next and then onto the next, not remaining in any reality for any length of time. I saw glimpses of myself and people I've met and know doing interesting and varied things.

I would liken the experience to taking LSD, ecstasy and psychotropic drugs and going on one heck of a weird ride, for want of a better way of explaining it. (In truth I've always avoided taking any kind of drugs, due to an intuitive sense that my body would not do well under the influence.) While having this disorientating experience it was difficult to focus on my client. Instead I strongly felt the need to mentally recite my phone numbers. Of course, I couldn't remember them, which created considerable inner stress. My concern was that I was having a major mental health episode of some kind.

While going through this experience I continued to remind myself that everything was all right, that I was not losing my marbles and that something energetic was happening. Hell, I didn't have a clue as to what was going on but somehow I knew that this was not a psychotic episode. The unexpected onset and intensity of this experience was significantly strong for me to realize that there was something happening energetically.

Much to my surprise I was able to drive home though it required inordinate concentration as I wasn't able to recall my address or mentally conjure up the route for the drive home. Once home I found both phone numbers written down on some papers and spent a lot of time memorizing them. It was as though I'd never seen them before! As I was doing this more of my memory returned. It was not just phone numbers that had escaped into the ether; it was also a significant portion of my memory.

Not surprisingly, I was disinclined to meditate or enter any surreal state for about a week or more after this unsettling episode. However, I was slowly able to glean information that a part of my brain had 'opened'. This part, which I'm unable to identify, is not usually opened in humans. In the following weeks I became aware of a new ability to see just about everything and to access an inordinate amount of universal information. When having a regular conversation with someone I would suddenly begin channelling relevant information and then revert to regular conversation. All intuitive faculties improved dramatically. (Journal, December 2011)

Reality Creation

So far I've shared my understanding of energy, its power, structure and potential, which I've attempted to explain in as straightforward a manner as possible. This information has been largely gleaned from channelling, clairvoyance experiences as well as from the teachings of non-physical beings that have been my constant companions. The journal entry at the beginning of this chapter is about energy, and describes one of the countless weird and unusual experiences I've encountered over a period of nearly thirty years. It was merely one of numerous incidents with energy changes, its impact and which also furthered my experience of the inexplicable. In the next chapter I've included a channelled explanation of what had taken place energetically within my energy hologram at another time as a result of an energy influx. Each energy influx is different, as each has a different function or purpose.

This may give you a better idea of what transpires when an energy download, or upgrade, occurs. The terms "energy download" or "upgrade" are interchangeable and are used to signify an energy change, or improvement, has occurred. They are a common occurrence for individuals who are continually on a personal journey of inner growth and spiritual awareness. In many instances they occur during sleep time which means that conscious awareness of this happening is likely to be limited or non-existent.

The other aspect of this is that everyone is special in their own way. My experiences are unique to me and are part of the package that I signed up for prior to incarnating into this lifetime. Whatever I have chosen to be part of is planned and orchestrated by my inner higher wisdom, or soul. It is not the same as what you've chosen to experience in this lifetime though there may be similarities in my sharing that you are able to relate to. I've learned that often simply sharing my unusual energy situations has helped others better understand and accept what has taken place within their energy hologram.

Nevertheless you may be interested in learning more about how to amplify and magnetize energy constructively in your life. My explanations are basic and can be viewed from a more practical, maybe even relevant perspective in everyday life. Therefore I'm going to branch briefly into a more logical explanation and description as that may further support and enhance understanding.

According to the science of physics, including quantum physics, the physical world is a large mass of energy that materializes and dematerializes continuously. Nothing is solid, it is our co-created perceptions that create whatever we perceive and believe. Quantum physics shows that the world is not constant. It is in continual motion (wave form energy) due to individual and collective thoughts that continually change and shape our reality. According to quantum physics it is this mass of thoughts that is responsible for holding this energy field (our reality) together in a cohesive yet ever changing state.

Each of the five physical senses has a particular range, which creates images and perceptions of reality. However, your interpretation and understanding of reality are based on an inner landscape that can be attributed to the sum total of your life experiences up to any particular point in time. This means that there exists a degree of fluidity and variation in reality perception and creation. In turn this depends upon your individual inner reality, which is continually being created via thought. As well, your personal inner reality is also part of the larger collective experience due to the energy interconnectedness of everything. Sounds complicated? The theory of it is complex yet it can be broken down into simple steps and explanations.

I happened upon a straightforward description online at http://consciousreminder.com. It refers to the human body as a means of explaining succinctly how this energy functions. The human body consists of nine different physical systems, including circulatory, endocrine, digestive, respiratory, etc. These systems are made up of tissue and organs, which in turn are made up of cells. The cells are made up of molecules, which are made from atoms. An atom is made up of subatomic particles, which in turn are made from energy.

This energy has been found to exist in every living organism – humans, animals and plants. It is visible at certain frequencies and is often evident to individuals with clairvoyant abilities. It is commonly referred to as light energy and is an intelligent configuration, constantly changing on subtle levels due to the power of thought. According to science you are made up of clusters of energy that continually shift and change. In other words, nothing remains constant or static. You are energy in continuous motion, always have been and always will be.

Quantum science has clearly demonstrated that simply an act of observing an object actually causes the object to be there. It also states that nothing that is observed is unaffected by the observer. This has been scientifically verified, thereby disproving the concept of objectivity in research. This is an important point to note. Objectivity cannot, and does not, exist in research according to quantum science. This means that the energy of the researcher impacts the outcomes of any scientific studies undertaken. Another way of expressing this is that everyone sees a different truth because everyone is creating what they perceive. It's not a case of believing what you see but seeing what you believe!

Everything I share in my writing is based upon my truth, which is simply a formation of my perceptions and experiences I have created up to this point in time. These have all occurred due to the power of thought. Every experience and insight I share has been interpreted and manifested through the filters of my consciousness. Along the way I've also acquired the skill of being able to access universal consciousness. This enables me to attract whatever is required at any one time in order to create or manifest into form (via words) whatever is intuitively needed. The art of being a writer is indeed a complex process when looked at in this manner!

In a channelled message received in 2001 this piece of information was shared:

> "When there are many of you resonating on the same wavelength with your thought forms and sending them all out to the cosmos they in turn come back and impact on the whole. In time those thoughts will filter through to others and this is how you create much of that which you believe and hold so dear. That being the case it could be argued that on your planet at this time the group consciousness that condones, accepts violence and killing and destruction has the upper hand. It is what is shaping your reality, for that is what the larger consciousness does. It impacts, not just on you, your family and neighborhood but on nations and globally of course.
>
> How much of what you see and hear about your world fills you with anxiety and dread? How often do you express your abhorrence of warfare, of viciousness? In many instances when you do it is a short-lived outburst. It is an outburst that is a reaction to a situation that has occurred. Because it has been brought to your attention, usually by the media, for a short while you express outrage. You become consumed with anger and fear thereby generating more of that. Emotions that you experience when you have a reaction to something violent or horrific are also sent out and are stored within the group consciousness. This in turn comes back and impacts all. It is a vicious cycle, is it not? It is one in which you are the co-creators."

What is Thought?

In the beginning there was the word. This is a familiar saying, and one that everybody has heard of, possibly with some variation, at some stage in life. You may have momentarily wondered about the deeper meaning of this, and then let it go. For many years I thought no more of it until my interest in energy began to seriously consume a lot of time, thought and study. I found myself asking numerous questions such as: "Where does thought come from?" "What is thought?" "How is it moved?" "Where does a thought go?" "What is mind and how does it work?" and "What is the nature of thought?"

These basic questions alone are sufficient to generate extensive philosophical pondering and discussion. I'm not a philosopher, nor inclined to engage in deep mental exploration and explanation for extended periods. My preference has always been to engage experientially, as this has been my most effective learning method over the years. However, during a meditation session nearly twenty years ago I received a significant amount of information about the nature of thought in a few seconds. Below, described as succinctly as possible is a summary of this information. As you've probably figured out by now I prefer simplicity, not complicated details, when it comes to exploring and discussing new information. My mind immediately grasps concepts without extensive language being needed. I sense concepts in a fraction of a second irrespective of their level of difficulty. The challenge is then to transcribe the concept into regular language.

- Thought is energy. It moves along the energy grid/matrix (hologram) system. All thought has vibration, though the vibration of thought is not of an even consistency. Low order thoughts have a lower vibration than high order thoughts. The vibration held by a thought will direct it to other thoughts of a similar nature or frequency, whether within the energy hologram of an individual or to the larger mass of energy consciousness. When sufficient thoughts of a similar vibration are pooled they then manifest into that particular vibration field. This is especially relevant to your ability to create and to manifest, both consciously and unconsciously.

- Thought alone holds a specific level of vibration. As a spoken word it also holds a similar vibration. When emotion is added to the thought/word then there is a further refinement or amplification of that vibration. For example, a thought about a person that is without any emotion will have a different vibrational charge than a thought holding an emotional component. Emotions strengthen the vibrational charge of a thought. Emotions can empower a thought positively or negatively. When emotions are attached to thought then the manifestation process is accelerated, especially when there is greater consistency of energy focused toward a particular area.

- Where does thought come from? This is a nebulous question and the answer may not be as clear-cut or concise as you may think. However, the simplest way of explaining is to say that there exists a limitless volume of thought forms already circulating within the larger mass consciousness. Access to this mass consciousness is readily available to everyone. Most people are unaware of the extent of their potential connection to this mass consciousness. This link exists due to the fact that absolutely everything exists within an energy framework and is connected and interconnected on all levels. This invisible energy wave form can just as easily be referred to as the web of life.

- When energy vibrates at a high frequency consistently it can easily be formatted into whatever manifestation is chosen through the thought/mind intention processes. You are a powerful creator and have the ability to manifest absolutely anything and everything. This is what you are continually doing, though in most instances this is happening unconsciously and often in a haphazard manner.

- Individuals are programmed with the capability to create thought, and to be receptive to fleeting concepts that come from within the soul essence or higher self. The soul is the seat of your connection to All That Is and contains a wealth of knowledge, wisdom and skills that your conscious (ego) mind usually is unaware of. This is energy of a higher order and when you aspire to live with meaning and connection to a higher source (spiritually) you are able to tap into the higher order consciousness.

Several concepts contained in the information above bear further comment. Firstly, the statement that thought is energy cannot be stressed highly enough. Consistently, my friends in non-physical form have reiterated that the human energy hologram contains the totality of memory from all lifetimes. This means that every thought and emotion is retained within the energy hologram, some stronger and others weaker in intensity. Also, every thought directed at others is held within, meaning that thoughts are like boomerangs. While they may affect others, they also impact the individual directing those thoughts and emotions. For example, having a negative thought about someone actually means that the intention and vibration of that thought remains within the individual holding that perception. This in turn remains within the individual's hologram, holding the specific frequency of that particular thought until such time that healing of lower order thoughts and emotions occurs. There is a good reason that the old adage, "If you can't say something nice then don't say anything at all" was widely touted by parents and grandparents. Words and thoughts have power!

In his well-documented research on the levels of human consciousness, David Hawkins, MD, PhD in his book, *Power Vs Force*, explores the relationship between thoughts, emotions and the body's responses. He states:

> "The connection between mind and body is immediate, so the body's responses shift and change from instant to instant in response to one's train of thought and the associated emotions…. When the mind is dominated by a negative worldview, the direct result is a repetition of minute changes in energy flow to the various body organs….. We could say that the invisible universe of thought and attitude becomes visible as a consequence of the body's habitual response."

When using muscle testing to determine the level of response Dr Hawkins found that high order thoughts recorded strongly within the body. Similarly, low order thoughts resulted in a weakened response when muscle tested. Likewise, my clients report feelings of wellbeing when they use positive and uplifting thoughts and emotions. However, when thoughts focus on negative life experiences the resultant perception changes to one of despondency, sadness and generally low feeling moods.

According to Torkom Saraydarian in his comprehensive tome, *Thought and the Glory of Thinking*:

> "Changes in our life must come through the changes in our consciousness. Those who want to improve their life, work on improving their thinking. They try to purify and focus their thinking, and the outer life follows the change….. Knowledge is mental food. Reading or listening to great ideas nourishes the body if one meditates on them, mentally understands them, and tries to live them."

This point is especially important. All too often it is easy to complain and express dissatisfaction with all that transpires in your life, as though life has singled you out for struggles, pain and suffering. In reality, nothing changes until your thinking changes. I will repeat that statement: *"Nothing changes until you change your thinking"*. This is a fundamental and core truth, one that is generally overlooked in the hurly-burly of daily life. You and only you have the power to change your thinking. It's your responsibility to create desired changes. There is no fairy godmother who's going to come along, wave a magic wand, and do it for you. Most people find that changing thinking is an extremely challenging undertaking. It is common to hear people say that their mind continues its endless and unremitting chatter of its own volition. Included in my sharing there are some suggestions that may support you in making changes to thinking processes and thought patterns if you feel dissatisfied with any aspect of your life.

Ultimately the aim is to become fully aware of, and responsible for, all thoughts and emotions you emit. In other words, this means that you organize universal energy into constructive reality creation, thereby reducing and eliminating the erratic consequences of undisciplined thoughts. Constructive reality creation can be achieved by disciplined action and commitment to manifesting desired changes.

Naturally many thoughts automatically revolve around matters relating to daily functioning. The mind has been trained or conditioned to continually focus on the numerous mundane details that vie for attention. Generally, some thoughts are conscious thoughts, meaning that they originate from issues and concerns that appear to be held in the conscious mind. In actuality they may be triggered by the subconscious memory. It is common, or normal, for there to be a myriad of repetitious thoughts flitting through your awareness day after day. Becoming aware of them and eliminating repetitive and contradictory thoughts is an ideal place to start making changes. The constant repetition of a thought pattern results in some degree of subconscious programming, which in turn has the potential to create a mind shift – for better or worse.

In the previous chapter I shared the benefits of focused breath work. It is the one technique I have found to be consistently successful in shutting down that constant barrage of inconsequential mind chatter. The more consistently and frequently I undertook this practice the more I became aware of an invisible barrier that separated my awareness from those unwanted thought intrusions. My body relaxed, felt stress free and there was both emptiness and silence within. This does not mean that the subconscious thoughts, masquerading as important conscious thoughts, have been eliminated. It simply means that there's an energetic shift occurring, one where your focus is fully in the present moment. The more I undertook this practice the greater the improvement.

Word Impeccability

The Four Agreements authored by Don Miguel Ruiz unearths and explores limiting beliefs and behaviors that prevent you from living a joyful, fulfilling life. Those particular convictions often create needless and ongoing suffering in life. The four agreements are based on ancient wisdom imparted via the Toltec civilization, and are straightforward guidelines for living impeccably. They are:

1. Be impeccable with your word;
2. Don't take anything personally;
3. Make no assumptions; and
4. Always do your very best.

Each agreement is basically a simplistic way of summarizing complex reasons for, and benefits of, living an impeccable and mindful life. As easy as that may sound, though not necessarily as easy to follow through, I have been a strong advocate for adhering to those four easy to remember statements in everyday life. In addition, I've adhered to *The Fifth Agreement* (published at a later date), of continually giving gratitude, since discovering the incredible power of gratitude and appreciation to transform and sweeten life.

What does being impeccable with your word actually mean? How can it be implemented? Why is it important? How it is beneficial? Before exploring these questions and discussing the reasons for this concept probably being one of the most challenging, I'm reminded of the work of Dr Emoto, and his remarkable research into the power of words.

The research by Dr Masaru Emoto, as outlined in his ground breaking book *The Healing Power of Water* unfortunately has largely been overlooked by other scientists and lay people alike. The ramifications of his research are far-reaching in everyday life, and the inherent message about the influence of both high and low frequency words on the body seems to have been widely understated or ignored.

In his comprehensive research Dr Emoto studied frozen water crystals and their response to specific emotions. He simply attached a word to each slide of frozen water in the experiment. Words covering a whole gamut of emotions such as love, hate, joy, sadness were written on a tag and attached to each ice crystal and left for a set period of time. Using magnification Dr Emoto's research clearly demonstrated the different impact of high and low frequency words on the ice crystals. High frequency words (love, kindness, gratitude) when viewed under a microscope expanded and looked as though they were flourishing. They were stunningly beautiful. The opposite occurred with low frequency words, which shrivelled dramatically due to the negative connotation (hate, dislike, ugly, horrible).

Given the fact that fluids comprise more than two-thirds of the human body it's easy to see and understand the impact on human physiology when it's fed an undiluted barrage of negative thoughts and emotions. A constant diet of negative, derisive words will invariably result in some form of impact on health. Cells contain water and when starved of love, joy and other high frequency words those cells begin to shrivel and the likelihood of some form of illness manifesting increases. This is a slow, steady process of health attrition.

Dr Emoto's research demonstrates clearly the power of words to influence health and wellbeing, both positively and negatively. Sadly, western culture ignores the importance of words/thought, with little or no focus on teaching mindfulness of thought in the education system or within the wider society. Spiritual teachers, however, are well versed and aware of the need for impeccable and immaculate speech. Enlightened souls throughout the ages have shared the inherent wisdom of using simplicity, preciseness and clarity of thought/word.

Words, Thoughts, Meaning And Consequences

The study of word origins and meaning is sadly omitted in most western education systems. While this subject may appear to be somewhat dry, uninteresting and uninspiring it is nevertheless quite the eye opener in regards as to actual language usage and its often unintended consequences. Language is dynamic. It continually changes and evolves. The language used today no longer resembles language usage of even one or two centuries ago. Reputable dictionaries such as the Oxford Dictionary continually add new word inventions to their hefty tome, thereby demonstrating clearly that language is a living experience.

Since developing acute awareness of the impact words have on my body and on the life I choose to craft I've found it easier to create and manifest constructively in all areas of my daily life. As a result, there are definite no-nos when it comes to vocabulary usage. Some basic words that I avoid are "want, try, hate, should, must" in addition to other ambiguous non-assertive words. Rather than proceeding into a full analysis for my reasoning I'll limit my explanation to the extent that I trust you'll find helpful and relevant. Here I stress, again, the importance and necessity of language mindfulness as a means of working constructively with energy in order to achieve greater ease and flow in life, wherever possible.

The word "want" means 'lack of, scarcity' so every time you think or say that particular word you are literally confirming lack and enhancing that scarcity energetically. There is no scarcity in the universe, yet it's created constantly through a focus on deficiency, including the constant use of that particular word "want". Whether you think or say it aloud there is no difference. You are magnetizing the energy of lack with continued use of this extremely over-used word. I'm always amazed when shopping to hear young children continually say, "I want…" The relentless repetition of this word is epidemic within our culture, and adults as well as young children are deeply indoctrinated into its usage. It's no wonder that there's so much perceived lack and scarcity in our co-created reality.

If you are wondering about positively charged energy words that can be used instead, how about using affirmative beginnings to your statements instead? Some effective examples include, but are not limited to: I have, I intend, I do, I plan, I am. A sentence commencing with the positive energy of "I do, have, am…." energizes your body due to its subtle response on the cellular and energetic levels. Action words (verbs) following "I" affirm strength and power in a positive manner.

"Try" is one of those words that means never succeeding. Why would you try when it's possible to succeed or create great outcomes? You either do or don't, it's as simple as that. Avoid the word "try" like the plague. When asserting positively with statements such as "I am… I do… I plan… I create…" you place an intention that carries a strong, affirmative energy. Trying simply means remaining in limbo, some place between doing and not doing and of course never creating desired or anticipated outcomes.

How often do you hear someone say "I hate it when….." The word "hate" is in constant use in everyday vocabulary and is deemed to be a widely acceptable means of expression. The research by Dr Emoto, based on water's response to words should be sufficient to warn you off from ever using that particular word again. The energy of the word "hate" impacts every cell in your body. When it's repeated, mindlessly many times per day, it has a cumulative impact that is detrimental to physical, mental and emotional health. Instead there are other words that can express displeasure, and which are not detrimental to your health and wellbeing. My personal favorites are "I choose…." or "I prefer…" as this changes the tone and energy of whatever is expressed. Ultimately, the ideal is to aspire to a state of non-judgment where observation without criticism ensures that your health and vitality are in no way negatively impacted.

"Should" "must" and "ought" are other words that can easily be eliminated from your vocabulary. They denote obligation and with that the underlying emotion is guilt. The energy of both obligation and guilt are what I refer to as being heavy. They denote a burden and unwillingness. Any words that impart feelings of less than, guilt, shame, regret and all the lower frequency emotions can be omitted from regular and daily use.

"But" is a useful though tricky conjunction, which is used to string two or more thoughts together. The downside to using "but" is that it comes between two separate ideas or concepts and it negates the first. As an example, in the following sentence the word "but" fully negates or dismisses the intention of the first part of the sentence. "She was really well behaved but managed to spoil it at the last minute." Instead of using "but" I prefer to separate the two distinct thoughts into two sentences so that each sentence has its own frequency. Doing this begins the process of reducing judgment and criticism. Even better is the ability to maintain the philosophy of looking for the best in everyone and everything – as challenging and difficult that may be at times!

As mentioned earlier, words hold frequency. A thought on its own holds a specific energy. When it's combined with an emotion that specific energy frequency amplifies. When that thought is repeated constantly the emotion intensifies even more with the resultant outcome often being the exact opposite of what is actually desired. It's common to observe people getting more of the same, when their deepest desire is actually to manifest different and positive outcomes. It's not a case of "Be careful what you wish for". It's a case of being impeccable with your words. That is the power of word/thought.

It is common to have unconscious conflicting energy emitted through daily word usage. Saying one thing and feeling its opposite results in counter-productive energy flow. For example, complimenting a person on their hair or appearance while actually thinking they look horrible results in mixed energy outcomes. The ideal is to ensure that thoughts, spoken words, emotions and actions all align with the same frequency and intention as that creates the greatest energy alignment and power.

Aligning thoughts, words, emotions and actions sounds simple and straightforward. It's actually quite challenging to put into practice consistently. Maintaining mindfulness of words (and language) requires continual diligence of what is used and applied, situation by situation.

A significant degree of self-analysis and willingness to explore possible options and changes are also required.

When I first became aware of my particular short-comings in word usage I asked certain friends to monitor my language. They became my word police! It was necessary to be reminded, often brutally, when my aspirations fell short. Whenever this occurred, and it happened often, it provided an opportunity for me to analyze language usage, its context, and to also begin formulating more appropriate responses. The whole process literally involved re-thinking my language structure and word usage so that greater alignment of energy could be achieved. It became an ongoing process of making adjustments and learning to listen to my body's responses to the words I used indiscriminately. This whole process requires a complete letting go of what has become automatic thought and speech responses in order to have conscious and mindful expression at all times.

Body Talk

Body talk works two ways. The body communicates with you and you also continually provide input and information, via thoughts and emotions. Remember that your body is an energy hologram, which means that your physical body cannot exist without ongoing energetic input into its perfectly attuned system. Every word/thought affects your body and simultaneously your body continually communicates with you on subtle levels. Annette Noontil in her book *The Body is the Barometer of the Soul* highlights clearly the many messages transmitted, usually via distress, pain or discomfort that is occurring in the body. Understanding your body's messages is the first step in gaining awareness via body talk. Your body is like a massive computer system, with ongoing communication networks functioning day and night in order to keep it in optimal condition. As soon as there is a minor glitch in the system there are sensitive alerts that kick off, sending messages via the many communication channels that something is awry or not functioning as it's meant to. Learning to hear what your body is saying requires time and plenty of practice.

Ultimately one of the most accurate and effective ways of determining the appropriateness of language is by feeling your body's response to words. In his research Dr David Hawkins MD PhD used muscle testing to determine the body's subtle energy response to specific words and phrases. Muscle testing is easily learned and has the potential to help you rapidly understand which words weaken and strengthen your body. For example, "sorry" weakens whereas "apologize" strengthens; "hate" weakens and "love" strengthens; and "please" weakens. Instead of "please" which like "sorry" places you in a position of subjugation to another person I found that "thank you" and "apologize" are a far more positive response. However, not everyone is familiar with muscle testing and often it's not convenient to take the time to check.

In order to determine whether a word or phrase is beneficial or detrimental I use the simple but effective body response mechanism as an indicator. For example, when I hear a word or about something that feels off or negative my stomach clenches slightly. This is a rapid response that passes through briefly and can easily be overlooked if my mind is focused elsewhere. A positive response is usually a warm, fuzzy feeling around my heart center. A neutral response is a distinct lack of feeling anything.

The more sensitive you are to the subtle non-physical energies the more likely you are to feel that brief, fleeting energetic response. However, not everyone is sensitive to subtle energies. In situations like this I suggest that it's possible to gradually shift that heavier energy within. I realize that heavier energy sounds somewhat judgmental. It's not. It's simply that there's often a great deal of mental, emotional and spiritual pain stored within from many lifetimes that results in energy density or heaviness. This sits within the chakra energy system and carries energy weight. At this stage it's unnecessary to explore and explain the importance of ensuring your chakra system is cleared of stagnant energy. However, if you've been neglecting this vital aspect of energy health I recommend that you begin undertaking the regular clearing out of old emotions, memories and other dated beliefs.

A simple technique that I was guided to undertake daily, which assisted in aiding sensitivity improvement and also supported chakra clearing greatly enhanced my ability to engage in body talk. I was guided to sit still, in a meditative state, and to visualize a stream of gold energy coursing through my crown chakra. This golden stream gradually moved down my body, clearing out the chakras and also supported the healing of pain spots in my body. In most instances there were energy blockages and pain aspects in parts of my body that I wasn't consciously aware of. As this golden energy slowly moved its way down, like gently falling rain, and encountered a blockage or pain spot I'd tune into it and attempt to figure out and understand what was happening. Surprisingly after a while I became quite adept at hearing what my body was telling me. Yes, it took commitment and practice. It was well worth it, as nowadays it's simply a matter of tuning into an area of discomfort and asking what it means. Most times the answer is not immediate. Later it pops into awareness at the most unexpected of times though.

Another aspect of body talk that's extremely important is how you talk to your body. This includes your thoughts and feelings about it. Saying "I love you" and making other affirmative statements to your body is crucial to overall health and wellbeing. Unfortunately we live in a culture that idealizes a certain body image, one that is never enough, never sufficiently perfect and always lacking in some way or shape. Feeding your body with massive doses of self-affirmation, love, gratitude and appreciation is potent energy food.

Practicing and learning self-love is critical to ensuring alignment with your highest good. If this one important aspect of self-growth is overlooked then the lack of self-love will always be the trigger that impedes the flow of abundance, wellness and health. Words/thoughts are the energy critical to manifestation and to the process of creation. At the same time the journey to self-acceptance and self-love may be one of the most challenging in your life. Any lack of self-love will prevent you from becoming a fully self-actualized person.

Understanding energy, its potency and the ramifications for working constructively with your beautiful energy hologram are the building blocks towards attaining a state of self-actualization, a term coined by Maslow. His work and its relevance to energy, frequency and vibrations will be explored further in a later chapter.

Chapter 8

Initially I felt a strong tingling sensation on the right side of my body. This soon became widespread. There were areas around my head where I felt more intense sensations. The energy also swirled throughout my whole being, completely adjusting my energy body on practically every level. Though I remained still it felt as though my body was rolling backwards and forwards. By this stage the whole experience was electrifying as energy coursed through my body like an electrical current.

Next I was impelled to place both hands, palms upwards, on the table. Then I experienced intense sensation of something moving through both index fingers. In time that sensation merged through the whole hand and then up my arms. The energy was vibrant and it became even stronger until such time each hand felt as though it was about ten times its actual size. There was definitely something in my palms! The whole experience lasted about fifteen minutes and when it finished I walked upstairs feeling somewhat refreshed yet relaxed simultaneously. (Journal entry, 2005)

*****

"There was much work done last night. We are proud of our efforts. You would not recognize your form due to the structural changes that have been made. The changes will settle in a few days' time and you will find your physical strength increased along with stronger balance. The new vibration is of a color that you do not yet have on your planet. Its tone is to assist your body in the assimilation of the frequency waves that connect us to you. This connection is essential for several reasons. Our communications will be easier, meaning you will find greater clarity in understanding our words. Simultaneously we will access your frequency easily with this improvement in technology.

You question about your hands. They are the means by which we have inserted this technology. There is no physical damage to your body, though you will benefit from relaxing your body until full adjustment occurs. There will be improvement in your physical energy levels and strength. Stamina will flow effortlessly from you when this process is fully established and stabilized. Improvements in your healing work will also result, with faster results becoming evident. Your new energy frequency is different to that of those around you and you may experience a minor subtle shift in people's perceptions as you enter their field, it too will settle in time. There is more to be added to our structure and you will know when to be still. We ask that you honor this process by not exerting your physicality too much for a few days after each supplementation. This way integration will be fairly smooth and comfortable for you. " (Channeling, explaining energy upgrade)

Cause and Possibility

As a human being you are extremely powerful. You are made up of ever-changing clusters of energy, moving in harmonious wave form arrangement. This constant wave motion is a function of thought and emotion. Metaphysics refers to the influence and power of the body, mind and spirit (soul) interconnection. The body is continually being created and modified due to thought and emotion, which can also be referred to as the 'cause'. Everything is created and manifested from thought!

Your body is capable of both experiencing and being the experience, or the object of your thoughts and emotions. This is unique to you and your observations, experiences and perceptions. Thought, however, is unable to experience. Thought creates, manifests and interprets and needs the body in order to experience. Underpinning this interconnectedness between body and thought there is the spirit/soul. It is through soul that everything functions and evolves. Soul gives meaning and provides opportunities for growth and deeper understanding and wisdom.

At some stage in evolution humans were also extremely connected to universal consciousness, in much the same manner animals and plants are. The ability to connect telepathically and instantaneously with all living beings was automatic and even considered normal once upon a time. This is an ability that over time eroded from human consciousness. I prefer to think of this ability as lying dormant, awaiting the ideal conditions in order to once again surface and strengthen.

According to the information that came through when I channelled the energy of the soul that embodied as Edgar Cayce humanity is currently undergoing an evolutionary leap. This leap is due to changes occurring within what science has referred to as junk DNA. According to Edgar there's no such thing as junk DNA. It's actually pieces of DNA embedded within the human genome and genetics awaiting the opportunity to once again be activated. The activation process entails the shift in awareness and increasing consciousness currently occurring in a co-created reality. Junk DNA, when activated, supports the evolutionary process from current low density at the global level into human light body manifestation and functioning. With this shift, once again the ability to communicate energetically with all that is living is awakened. Perhaps with time the ability to communicate verbally will become obsolete or redundant. Maybe it's even possible that widespread communication with animals and plants will also become commonplace.

The subject of telepathic or energetic communication has been extensively explored by Grazyna Gosar and Franz Bludorf in their book *Vernetzte Intelligenz* (Networked Intelligence), available only in German. This research information was shared on http://consciousreminder.com and I'm including it to demonstrate the validity of information shared by my non-physical friends over a period of some years. Gosar and Bludorf, and other researchers interested in exploring the real potential of DNA have confirmed the full potential of super communication between life forms, the processes involved and also the long-term potential. The means by which they maintain this possibility is through the probability of the junk DNA being activated. The activation of this potential is dependent upon the extent to which inner work is undertaken by you, individually and collectively. It is through the individual inner work undertaken that the greatest strides can be made and progress attained. Your DNA reacts and responds to language. Hence word usage and context become increasingly important in supporting and creating your shift into higher awareness.

For years I've likened the human body to a computer, maintaining that beliefs, perceptions, conditioning and so on have been programmed via recurring life situations. If something has been programmed then surely it can be reprogrammed. This point is especially important as it has been demonstrated that the power of affirmations, meditation and giving gratitude all have the potential to produce positive outcomes. Engaging in these simple wellness practices is part of the reprogramming process. As a professional I've encouraged clients to use the power of thought (intention) as a healing tool. Visualization, affirmation and gratitude are powerful tools and are not only beneficial for healing illness conditions. They are invaluable for optimal health and wellbeing creation, including the manifestation of desires and purpose.

Reprogramming Thinking

The programming you hold within is located within the framework of your particular energy hologram. This programming refers to all the beliefs, patterns, perceptions, thoughts, trauma, emotions, and so on that occur continuously throughout each lifetime that is experienced. Unfortunately, if you are one of those souls that has experienced an unusually large number of lifetimes then it's likely your inner work requires greater commitment and mindfulness with the reprogramming process. Some individuals seem to get an easier ride through life than others. It's simply a matter of soul choice. Mine has certainly been challenging though nowadays I consider myself privileged to have survived and thrived. My rantings of frustration at non-physical friends has finally become a thing of the past.

When you dwell on a concept, worry, emotion, or issue constantly its energy charge, or vibrational frequency, strengthens. In time that particular thought becomes programmed into your energy hologram. However, the magic of this wonderful process of programming is that if you are dissatisfied with what you have created in your life you have the power and ability to reprogram the energy hologram.

One of the first steps to reprogramming thoughts is to actually become aware of the patterns of thinking you hold. The checklist of statements below will help you gauge the manner in which your thinking functions. Some of the statements may, or may not apply. If they don't then I suggest that you substitute ones that are relevant to you.

- "I find myself saying the same things as my mother/father always said." When you repeat the generational patterns of thinking then there may be emotions and thoughts that no longer serve your highest good. In fact, they may not actually be representative of your real beliefs. You may merely have internalized them as your own. Ask yourself, "Why do I say this?" "Do I believe this statement?" "Does this belief serve me now?" As you begin questioning your responses you will be surprised at the extent to which you have accepted as normal the beliefs that others have impressed, and imposed, upon you.

- "I have difficulty tolerating/accepting....." Here you may find you have numerous intolerances. All are worthy of closer scrutiny. Ask, "Why am I intolerant, or not accepting of this?" "Where does this intolerance originate?" "What is needed to release this intolerance?" As you delve into your intolerances you will find that there is an emotional charge every time you focus on whatever is unacceptable. In this instance it is important to also question the intensity of emotional reaction. In spiritual teachings, everyone you connect with is your mirror. When you interact with someone you have difficulty tolerating or accepting, they are showing you that you actually still have some of that trait within you. If your reaction is intense then you are strongly charged with that energy. On the other hand, if your reaction is either mild or one of observation then that particular energy is diminished within you.

- "I'm not good enough, talented enough, strong...." All those thoughts of inadequacy and limitation indicate an inherent belief in your unworthiness. This is a common belief, often stored on the subconscious level. Ask yourself, "Why do I feel this way?" "In what situations does this feeling surface?" "What is my earliest experience of feeling like this?" "Is there really any reason to feel this way?" "What can I do to change this belief?" When you are ready to let go of the inadequacy belief and change it to one of self-worth you will find the answers. Often they will emerge intuitively as an insight or a knowing. As you begin this process of healing thoughts of inadequacy and limitation you will most likely discover there are more than you initially identified. You are merely peeling away the layers, one at a time, in much the same way as you peel away the layers of the never-ending onion.

- "I can't change….." It's common to hear an individual say "I can't change who I am" or words with a similar meaning. Or, "I can't do….". Whatever you think is what you get. If your life is limited by the word "can't" it may be worthwhile reflecting on why this particular word holds the power to limit and control your life. Why do you believe that you can't do or achieve something? Where does this belief originate? How often is this belief reinforced? What situations provoke this response? There are only a few possible questions that may provoke a response. If that's the case then I encourage you to explore and dig deeper to find the core reason for this consistent thought pattern and response. You can be and do anything your heart desires.

- "It's too hard" or "It's tough". What you believe is what you get. At what stage in life did you begin feeling this way? Have you adopted this perspective because you've heard family members continually make these statements? When did you begin limiting your potential? Why do you fear success? There are countless questions that can be asked around this belief. It's your responsibility to begin unravelling the reasons for your reluctance to achieve. It may be an avoidance strategy. It may be a deep-seated subconscious fear. Or, it may be something entirely different.

A strategy I've found to be powerful is to actually re-frame limiting, negative thought patterns into their opposite. For example, using empowering statements beginning with words such as "I can…" "I do…", "I am…." has the potential for shifting outcomes into life changing opportunities. To enhance the vibration of the re-phrased thought I also visualize it happening, and then add the feeling associated with the positive, uplifting thought. For example, "I don't have the money for…." can be re-phrased as "I have the finances for…. plus more". This is a simple way of shifting from lack or difficulty into one of manifestation. The vibration of the statement "I have the finances for…" is vastly different to the one beginning with "I don't have the money for….". Read both statements again and feel the difference and become aware of how limitations are created through the use of words.

Generally, desired changes begin to become apparent within a month of reprogramming language usage. Initially changes may appear to be subtle and that's because the energy charge is still gaining momentum. With continued intention and application, the energy increases in intensity, which in turn enhances amplification and from there intensifies the manifestation of changes. The inner changes are often the most profound. Feelings of wellbeing and intense achievement are two indicators of increasing self-empowerment. The process of reprogramming is ongoing. It has the potential to be expanded and increased in scope on an ongoing basis. This arises as you become more aware of your ability to manifest and to be in alignment with universal energy flow.

There are many factors to be considered when changing language usage and discarding thoughts and words that impact negatively on your ability to live an empowered life. I have acquired the knowledge I'm sharing due to my own experiences over countless years of exploring and experimenting with word meaning and application. It must be remembered, this subject is vitally important as it is thought that continually manifests reality. It's my hope, that by the end of this book, you will be fully immersed in experimenting with word usage and consequently have begun to make relevant and supportive changes, as they relate to your desires and intentions.

Conscious Mind

Given that education systems in developed countries focus largely on left-brain dominance functioning it is no wonder that thinking, using logic and reasoning is the predominant means by which individuals operate. From an early age the emphasis is on developing intellect in young children, as the ability to think, rationalize, analyze and synthesize are the general determinants of an individual's success within society. The ability to think coherently, logically and analytically is highly valued, and this ability usually is a function of the conscious ego based mind.

The subconscious mind holds a wealth of information based on emotions, experiences from all lifetimes and embedded beliefs and values.

Subconscious thoughts continually percolate to the surface of consciousness, stamping thought processes with depth, meaning and emotion.

However, it is likely that the conscious mind often appears to be the dominant player in conscious thought creation processes. In most instances it is actually the subconscious programming that drives the conscious mind. When there is a persistent flow of thoughts continually surfacing in the mind, it indicates over-activity on the mental level of the energy hologram. This reflects an imbalance in the overall energy levels, whereas the ultimate aim of achieving wellbeing is to create balance in all areas of the human energy hologram.

Over ten years ago I received another relevant insight into the nature of thought. As you change your thoughts on the conscious level you also begin the process of reprogramming the subconscious mind. I've deliberately used the word "reprogramming" due to the fact that the human energy hologram can be likened to a computer because computer language is commonly used and understood in our culture. You are the sum total of all your experiences, continually inputting new data and feelings, thereby creating a program for your life experiences and direction. Being a powerful, dynamic energy being you actually have the ability to reprogram your energy hologram on an ongoing basis. If you are dissatisfied with the one you have already created then you have an opportunity to create a new reality landscape.

Subconscious Mind

When I think about the subconscious mind I think about an iceberg. One tenth is above water and nine-tenths is below water. I then ask what – conscious or subconscious mind - is likely to have the most influence on thoughts, beliefs, actions and so on? As explained earlier I have found the focused breath technique brilliant for stepping into a state of non-thought. Yet, does this emptiness of mind in any way impact the subconscious mind and its programming that has accumulated over countless lifetimes? Personally I doubt that it does to any significant degree. Being in a state of non-thought induces a space where the body feels as though there's no stress; it induces calm and also clear headedness. As the feeling of being clearheaded continues, time feels like it stands still. That feeling does not necessarily reprogram the subconscious mind of thoughts and memory that are no longer relevant. However, before proceeding to what the reprogramming process involves I feel it's important to gain more of an understanding, however basic, of the role and functioning of the subconscious mind. It's a vital part or component of the human psyche. It's neither good nor bad. It simply has a pivotal role to play in survival and instinctual responses.

Here I profess that my book knowledge of psychology is basic. It's not based on deep psychological studies despite the fact that one of my passions is learning about motivation, what drives individuals, and more. A great deal of what I know is gleaned psychically and also via channelled information. Regardless, I value whatever surfaces via my consciousness. I give it credibility and have come to understand that in the process of living many lifetimes it's possible, in this lifetime, to bring that knowledge to the fore of awareness whenever it's relevant or needed.

On a physical level the subconscious apparently has a role in keeping your body in a state of homeostasis. This means that it supports the regulation of your body's temperature, keeping it at 98.6 degrees Fahrenheit. It supports both breathing and heart rate and ensures they continue steadily. The subconscious works through the autonomic nervous system maintaining a state of balance among the chemicals in your body's cells. Overall the function of the subconscious is to also maintain harmony within your body. (From http://brian.tracy.com/blog/personal-success/understanding-your-subconscious-mind/) On the mental level it supports your thinking and actions that are consistent and in alignment with what's been happening previously. The subconscious mind triggers feelings and emotions, especially when it comes to undertaking something new and unfamiliar. The subconscious mind may trigger a trauma or fear based situation that's been held somewhere within the depth of its storage capacity. To my way of thinking, in keeping with the computer analogies, the subconscious could also be described as a super computer that manages the smooth functioning of its data.

The subconscious is like a massive storage container, holding memory of all lifetimes, emotions, beliefs, trauma and so on. There is nothing that has happened that has escaped spending time in the subconscious. That may make it sound more like a prison than a super computer. Another word that may be more appropriate is "repository". Being a repository implies that it's more like a massive warehouse where information comes in and goes out, and where the replacement of material (information) has the potential to be upgraded and changed.

The study of the conscious, subconscious and super conscious minds has involved years of study by professionals due to their interest in exploring and understanding human behavior and nature. That is not intended to be the case here. I'm interested in sharing in a simplified manner the power of thought/word as an energy within the subconscious, its impact and also its potential for creating conscious change and growth. Understanding the process involved, how it impacts you on the deeper levels and the potential for long lasting wellbeing and health is, I believe, both relevant and important.

Expressed most simply the subconscious:

- Records everything from all times;
- Is always alert and awake. That's part of its role in ensuring homeostasis and other bodily functions are maintained;
- Manages and controls approximately ninety-five percent of all that occurs in your life;
- Is built on a process of habituation. The more you do something the more ingrained as an instinctual response it becomes;
- Communicates to you via dreams. Often this is to remind you of something or to alert you when something needs your conscious attention;
- Lacks verbal language though it responds and functions energetically;
- Takes everything literally. This is a vital point and stresses the importance of being impeccable with your word;
- Has the ability to do millions of things simultaneously. This is the ultimate multi-tasking machine;
- Is not logical or literal. It is a feeling mind, operating from emotional responses; and
- Is significantly and vastly more powerful than the conscious mind.

At times I've seen clients whose energy hologram holds information that indicates deep trauma and/or pain memory. This trauma/pain memory holds a frequency and it's picked up intuitively or psychically. An individual may have absolutely no memory or even indication of anything untoward ever happening. Yet, on some level there's a feeling of inner disquiet, often extremely subtle. In my lay person terminology I refer to instances such as this as suppressed memory. It may have happened in another lifetime, in the womb or even in early infancy. In instances such as this hypnosis has the potential to support a process of healing. It's quite common for an individual to live in many lifetimes and to carry the memories of those lifetimes into the present moment. Those memories may surface unexpectedly and even vividly, causing discomfort and even distress.

Realistically trauma memories are energy that hold a specific frequency, which in most cases do not resonate with the frequency of the person experiencing those painful trauma memories. As I explain to clients, again and again, when this occurs it's old energy, old memories, that are releasing. They are working their way out through the many layers of the energy hologram. While it's happening there is a re-experiencing of some intense emotion. My non-physical friends and teachers insisted that simply expressing gratitude for the release is all that's needed to support the process. In a channelling it was explained that attaching worry, concern and stress over such a release process actually results in further stress and reality creation. This in turn intensifies the energy of the stored memory, further creating additional mind induced trauma.

Subconscious Functioning

It's possible to change and reprogram the subconscious mind over a period of time, and most likely it will be a prolonged period. This is a process that can proceed haphazardly or with some semblance of structure and order. My personal preference is a structured process, starting with the more obvious and straightforward and then gradually moving into the more complex and challenging. Another way of expressing this is begin with reprogramming whatever is most troublesome and annoying at the moment. Gradually over time, once the initial issues are no longer a problem you'll then become aware of other concerns, beliefs and memories that are no longer evident but which exist on a subtle level within your subconscious storage system – in much the same way that a virus slowly creates disruption in your computer's optimal functioning.

I'm including the rules of the subconscious mind as outlined by M. Farouk Radwan MSc at www.2knowmyself.com/subconscious_mind/ subconscious_mind_rules_power. The language used in this article is direct and geared toward the non-professional in the field, which is why I'm including it. The rules are:

- There is no differentiation between reality and visualizations. This is one of the reasons I'll often say to clients that simply visualizing or imagining something is powerful. It has the same impact and energy on the subconscious. This is why such things as Vision Boards and writing wish lists are helpful in manifesting change and positive outcomes.

- There's no sense of time with the subconscious. Actually time is a human, ego based construct, geared to control and manage you into predictable routine. The indigenous populations do not have the same construct of linear time, and are much more attuned to the Now moment. When asleep the subconscious remains awake while the conscious mind becomes dormant.

- It may take up to a month for the physical body to adjust and integrate a new technique of movement, such as in yoga. In the same way the longer the subconscious is fed the same or similar information the more it will settle and ultimately become more difficult to shift. This is one of the reasons that deep seated beliefs are often difficult to identify and release.

- Whatever you think or believe is what you'll get. There is a physical reaction or consequence to your thoughts and words. A simple example is the flu season and beliefs around it. Hearing people say, "Everyone in my family has the flu and I'll get it next" is a sure fire guarantee that it will happen. This is a classic example of the power of thought and the energy of creation it holds.

- Your expectations become reality. The realization of your expectations is abundantly evident in everyday society. Expect the worst and that's what will happen, especially when the subconscious is fed a diet of thoughts that support this creation. Expect and anticipate the best and the outcome is likely to reflect that expectation. There are exceptions to this and they relate to genetic blueprint, or soul plan set in motion prior to incarnating. However, overall this particular rule – expectations become reality – tends to be the norm.

- Whatever you believe is validated. For example, if you have body image issues then those beliefs will be reinforced by individuals in the outer reality.

- The subconscious mind is more powerful than the conscious mind. Telling yourself there is nothing to be afraid of, that you're quite safe is a conscious mind action. The inner, subconscious knowing based on experiences through lifetimes will override the conscious thoughts and intentions.

- Once an idea is accepted, either individually or on a larger scale, it will remain until there is another idea that supersedes it. As a collective there is some degree of comfort gained in being part of the larger mass. The firmer an idea is entrenched the more challenging it is for a new concept to take hold. An example of this relates to the work of Nikola Tesla. His early work in the field of the quantum sciences and its relevance is slowly making its way into the population at large. The quantum sciences are still undergoing a slow process of wider acceptance, despite the amazing and indisputable research findings he made about energy early last century.

- Consciously imposing or forcing change on the subconscious results in greater resistance. An example relates to giving up an addictive habit, such as excessive alcohol consumption. Consciously reiterating, "I don't need a drink" is more likely to induce greater craving. Instead, programs such as the Twelve Step program meet with success because the issue isn't about forcing change; it's about adopting changes slowly, gradually and incrementally.

- The subconscious mind can be programmed (or reprogrammed). Hypnosis is one technique that's been used successfully. Sending suggestions to the subconscious is a subtle way of releasing fears, habituation, beliefs and more and in the process desired change is created.

Reprogramming Subconscious Mind

When reprogramming of the subconscious mind occurs it is important to begin emptying the conscious mind of continual thought. Needless to say, meditation and focused breath work (explained previously) are highly effective means of eliminating or reducing distracting and time-consuming thoughts. As the conscious mind begins to clear itself of incessant chatter it becomes possible to hear the voice of the subconscious mind, which too can be released of old programs and beliefs. This is a process that requires both time and patience to master. Buddhist monks devote years to emptying the mind so the rest of us mere mortals need to remember to be both patient and kind to self when undertaking this journey.

Ultimately, the aim is to have both conscious and subconscious minds cleared of the distracting mindless and incessant chatter as much as possible. Clearing the subconscious takes longer because it relates to letting go of beliefs, fears and other stagnant energy. This, however can steadily be cleared through undertaking regular and committed inner work. Once the release and reprogramming happens then there is only the clarity of knowingness left within. This is the voice of the soul. It is the voice of eternal inner wisdom. When the soul is allowed full, clear and concise expression then and only then, is true enlightenment possible.

A statement by my friends in non-physical form expressed this possibility very clearly one day as I was driving in the midst of considerable traffic congestion in Seattle. Due to its significance I immediately memorized their statement and wrote it down as soon as possible. The words I clearly heard asserted were: *"Full empowerment of consciousness will only ever be realized when the voice of the soul is the expression of that consciousness."*

Creating a state where both conscious and subconscious minds are stilled so that the voice of the soul can be your main voice of expression is definitely worth aspiring to. The reality, however, is that the majority of the world's population is far, far from this ideal state. Instead, I believe that significant change can occur when small changes to thinking are made by an individual. It is not necessary, or desirable, to attempt drastic changes in a short period of time. Often I remind clients of the importance of practicing gentleness in their endeavours. I highly recommend that you also treat your endeavours with patience and joyfulness.

Begin with simple changes. Change your thinking. Become mindful of your thoughts and emotions. Ditch those that no longer resonate or feel right. Substitute them with thoughts that feel more appropriate to who you are now. One of the most recent, and powerful, pieces of advice I heard from my non-physical friends is to let go of your past. Don't hang onto beliefs or emotions that relate to your past. Let go of mementos that keep your mind, heart and energy focused on whatever has occurred in the past, regardless of how painful or wonderful they may be. This may be somewhat of a radical move. Letting go of the past may mean letting go of your foundations, your sense of self, your place in a community and so on. Yet, it's extremely valuable advice.

When I heard that particular piece of advice I intuitively saw a blank canvas, which represents a new start, an opportunity to create new desires and more. Then my awareness was drawn to the nature of snakes. Snakes shed their skin and the insight gleaned is that it's important for individuals, at this point in our linear time, to shed their old skin. It has no relevance in the new energies and frequencies that are bombarding the planet now. Snakes shed their skin because they grow a new skin, one that is more suited to their current needs. If snakes have this instinctual knowing and can do this intentionally then surely it's possible for humans to do the same through intention and motivation. The difference being that snakes shed a physical aspect of their being. You have the ability to shed energetically through conscious intention.

As your conscious mind commands a change in thinking your subconscious mind responds accordingly. Consciously using positive and uplifting thoughts, often in the form of mantras and affirmations, is an ideal tool for reprogramming subconscious mind. Another way is to read inspirational quotes, whether penned by a famous author or by your own hand. Write them down and read them frequently. You are then feeding your subconscious a new stream of consciousness. Create inspiring habits in your daily routine. Feed yourself loving words. Feed your body love and compassion on a daily basis. Write affirmative lists of your amazing skills, characteristics and attributes, and then read them often.

Two effective statements that I must have repeated a million times during periods of stress and uncertainty played an important role in the steady process of reprogramming my subconscious. The statements are: "This too shall pass" and "It is what it is". Whenever an issue or situation arose that I was uncomfortable with, or which had been stirred up by some subconscious memory I repeated either or both until there was a feeling of greater ease and comfort within. Over time I realized the power of these particular statements. By mentally saying or vocalizing the statements I was creating an energetic distance between whatever was sitting in the subconscious and the emotion/feeling attached to it. In some way I was dis-engaging from deep seated subconscious memory and creating a new way, a way of non-attachment to minor issues. On another note an issue is only minor or major when it's perceived that way. Simply by letting go of old memories, emotions and beliefs you are making space for new energies to fill that vacant space.

At the beginning of the last chapter I shared a journal entry from 2011 about an incident that created disturbance in my reality. At the time I was unsure as to the purpose of the unsettling experience. I put it off as one of those weird energy phenomena that have become commonplace in my life. Yet it wasn't weird or random. It was a gift, even though at the time I didn't recognize it as such. It was not until some years later I came to understand that I'd experienced a "memory erasure". While this sounds drastic I can assure you that it wasn't. It was simply like a blackboard being cleaned of old writing. Some higher wisdom, possibly my own, knew it was time to de-clutter my subconscious of extraneous memory. The benefit of this is that some subconscious programming, no longer vital to my wellbeing, was erased. Since then I've experienced further subconscious de-cluttering as needed, for which I'm deeply grateful.

Is this type of subconscious de-cluttering available to everyone? I truly do not know. Each individual has a unique self-designed path and purpose in this lifetime. Most likely subconscious de-cluttering has happened to other individuals though I have not been made aware of it happening. On the other hand it may have occurred as a paranormal energy experience due to the fact that my diligence in letting go of dated emotions, beliefs, fears, programs, and so on had reached a critical point where a subconscious de-clutter was possible. All I know is that the potential for constructive, uplifting change is possible when working with conscious intention is combined with a willingness to create change in life. I'm reminded of the old saying: "If you continue to do what you've always done, you'll get what you've always got". If nothing else, that fundamental statement should be sufficient motivation to get real about manifesting positive inner growth in order to be aligned with your purpose and path in this lifetime.

Chapter 9

I attended The Art of Living event, a six-day workshop experience. It was profound. The effects remain. Physically it feels as though my body has undergoing a complete shift. During the workshop, after a long breathing exercise we went into a meditation. It was guided, yet I wasn't participating. I found myself totally pulled elsewhere. It felt as though I was ensconced within a large rectangular box with my whole body feeling numb or anaesthetized. It was a lengthy meditation and I have no specific recollection of it. Overall it felt as though my whole energetic body was completely rearranged. Maybe new pieces were inserted and the old was removed. I cannot say with any certainty.

One day after this workshop as I was lying on the couch it felt as though a thin layer was peeled off my back. That night I had a dream experience. In that dream I was lying in bed, curled up in a foetal position, with the comforter pulled tightly around me. Something began to tug at the comforter. I held onto it, resisting the pulling. However, the pulling persisted and eventually I relinquished hold. It felt like something huge and major was pulled right off my back, somewhat like a tortoise losing its shell. Since then my back has felt totally different – it feels like a huge load has been lifted.

In the last few days I've felt wretched – feeling anger, rage, grief, despondency and a whole mix of emotions! It has not felt overly comfortable. According to a shaman friend I'm experiencing a spiritual death, and that's exactly what it feels like.

****

"Begin now to gather your thoughts. There will be moments of heightened awareness, greater lucidity and this will be intermittent for some time. Then will come the day when you will feel great awareness and lucidity. Many

thoughts and ideas will come together as if in a combustive state. You will feel great knowingness. This is the state you are working towards. As you well understand, there is much to learn and to master during this process. You are a great teacher, a master….yet it all has to flow effortlessly. So for now you are the student, being groomed for your rightful role. Now is the time of rehearsing or preparing. Your physicality must be up to the task that you've set for yourself. Mentally you are well grounded and prepared. Emotionally that is almost the same and spiritually you are indeed a warrior, for you will be treading a new path. This path is yours. There are none who will have the temerity to venture as far. Others too play their part and follow their destiny. Yours, however, is truly different. There will be times when you will feel great loneliness. Know this is your human conditioning. You are not alone, nor ever will be. Yours is not a normal human lifetime. At one stage you attempted to live in this manner and it was not to your suiting. In time it will feel less and less like a human lifetime for you. We are always with you. Encouraging, supporting and pushing you to achieve your endeavours." (Journal entry and automatic writing, 2005)

It has been nearly fifteen years since that energy layer was removed from my back, and the channelled message that followed it. Since that time there has been continuous and ongoing energy shifts and expansion occurring. Each time there is another energy shift it feels special and impactful. Yet, when viewed along the continuum of linear time this process of energy expansion into higher frequency and levels of consciousness appears to be a never ending process. With every minor or major shift I used to be convinced that this was it, that I had finally reached that ever so elusive pinnacle. Realistically, there is no pinnacle or destination to reach, it is a continuum. Further and ongoing refinement occurs, with each refinement feeling pivotal and momentous. The flashes of lucidity and insight continue to be clearer and sharper than ever before.

A spiritual death is often used as a descriptor of this process because it indicates that a massive inner shift has occurred. It's a letting go, or death of the old you. This generally is intensely uncomfortable and may even be painful. Subsequent to the experience of having an energetic shell, or layer, removed from my back in 2005 several intuitive insights popped into mind. They include:

- There are many levels to advancement in consciousness. A spiritual death is often referred to as a "dark night of the soul" and is one of the possible methods by which energy shifts occur. The dark night of the soul is usually an agonizing process, which may last for some time. This process is essential as it supports the peeling away of the outer and denser layers that have formed over lifetimes. The dark night of the soul assists you in gaining insight as to the nature of your real self. Questions such as, "Who am I? What am I really here for? What is my purpose?" are often the onset triggers to the dark night of the soul experience. This intense and harrowing process can last anywhere from a few days to months at a time.
- The dark night of the soul is literally a shedding of a vast amount of memory from the energy levels, within the energy hologram. This memory is stored deep within the cellular and energetic levels, within the DNA and genetic blueprint. This memory contains a mix of many things depending upon the individual. The common thread, however, is that the memory is usually from other times and places. This memory has some degree of density and as you seek increasing awareness or enlightenment there is a continual increase in vibrational frequency. This means that stored memory, vibrating at a lower frequency, is not in harmony with the new vibration (created by intention and thought). Therefore the lower frequency has to be sloughed off. The release of this memory is not a straightforward process, as it is cleared from the various energy levels. As the release occurs there is an attendant shift within the varying levels. They have to adjust and be realigned into a new and totally different energy hologram structure. This process is orchestrated at the electrical level, through the electrical pulsing that exists within the physical body. It permeates all levels and is the mechanism by which everything happens in your body.

As this process of ongoing and continuing energy refinement occurs heightened sensitivity becomes increasingly evident. What was once tolerable is no longer tolerated or acceptable. This is due to a lack of energy resonance. For example, it's most likely that certain people will no longer be part of your social group, you may change employment, dietary lifestyle most likely become cleaner and greener, relationships may change or wither, activities once enjoyed may no longer be fulfilling. The number of changes that occur may be minor or they may be significant, depending upon the extent of the frequency shift. This is all part of the process that you and others on the planet are currently undergoing. It's an amazing process. If for any reason you're experiencing discomfort and pain I assure you this is only temporary. Life certainly does improve and become sweeter.

Subconscious De-Clutter

As mentioned previously affirmations and other ongoing practices such as giving gratitude are powerful tools for de-cluttering the subconscious of stagnant energies and lower frequency memories, beliefs, trauma, and so on. There's no doubt that thought/word is the most effective method for creating shifts deep within. Some years ago I happened accidentally to come across simple, yet highly effective methods of de-cluttering the subconscious of extraneous and dated memory. As per usual, it happened during a fit of pique, where once again I'd decided that things were moving at snail's pace instead of galloping along. For some obscure and unknown reason the yearning to be green and clean on every level has been the inner impetus for shedding every layer of stagnant energy that I could possibly shed – as rapidly as possible!

I stated clearly, in a straightforward no nonsense manner, "I command that all that no longer serves my highest good, from all times, planes and dimensions be released with love". It's amazing what a succinct statement like that can achieve – again and again! For a day or two nothing happened. In fact, within a day I'd totally forgotten the stated intention. Next thing I felt out of sorts, with aches and pains on every level. My mood became dark, gloomy, angry, despondent and more. The sudden onset with which this occurred took me by surprise and mentally I asked, "What is happening and why?" The response in my head was pithy, "You asked for it". Had I really asked to feel so crappy and irate? While I didn't remember requesting those particular moods my memory went into overdrive and I went, "Oh, so I did". Not once did I ever consider stating that the process be gentle or kind to my body. After numerous experiences of commanding this type of clearing I realized that taking a gentle approach would have merely prolonged the period over which the stagnant emotions and energy were released.

The first time I commanded this type of energy clearing there was no awareness or understanding of its potential and power. Since that time the command has been made time and again, and my body's response varies each time, according to whatever energetic memory sits within and is ready to be released. Ironically, after a few days of dark, brooding moodiness there was a real shift with feelings of clarity, light heartedness and abundant energy flowing throughout the energy hologram.

As the energy hologram de-clutters stagnant energies there's also a flow-on effect into the subconscious. Reducing the stagnation on an energy level impacts the whole. This then creates an opportunity for further reprogramming of the subconscious mind via affirmations, loving intentions, gratitude and appreciation. It's literally a one-step-at-a-time process.

Cords of Attachment

The first time I encountered the concept of cords of attachment it related to a relationship that had ended. Surprisingly I still felt as though there was some lingering energy that was holding me back from moving on. What I learned from this particular incident is that throughout lifetimes you connect with all kinds of people, issues, beliefs and so on. Each of them lingers energetically if there's no complete letting go or detachment. Specifically I psychically saw a most interesting sight that explained this energy phenomenon perfectly. I saw an old-fashioned telegraph switchboard, as was common in the early years of the twentieth century. At that time all calls went through a telephonist, where you would specify the phone number and city of the person you wished to speak with. The telegraph operator would connect a plug to a point on the switchboard in order to put the call through. Psychically I saw a large switchboard and connected to it were countless cords, representing cords of attachment.

The cords varied in size, thickness and strength. Some were translucent and thin, like spaghetti strands. Others were weak. Others still pulsated strongly with energy.

The cords of attachment can be with loved ones, with your nemesis, a religious system, a belief about yourself and/or the world. In fact, anything that you have angst over or have become overly attached to, where you have expended a great deal of emotional energy could be the basis for the cord of attachment. The cords of attachment contribute to the clutter within your energy hologram, with the connection sitting within the emotional level along with triggers that remain in the subconscious.

In the situation where a relationship had ended I commanded that any and all cords of attachment between me and this person be cut with love. In my mind's eye I saw a pair of scissors cutting through the cord of attachment. At the same time I clearly heard (in my head), "Ow, what did you do that for?" My mental response was to thank him for our time together, and then to assert that both he and I needed to move on with our separate lives.

The next phase in my learning and understanding around cords of attachment occurred when I happened to psychically see a client's back, which was full of thin, feeble translucent cords. My immediate knowing was that the majority of these were from other lifetimes. Instead of cutting the cords I placed the intention to pull them all out, to unplug them permanently. Once that was completed I filled the whole back with gold light energy.

Nowadays I state, "I command all cords of attachment from all times, planes and dimensions be removed with love, with the exception of cords of attachment that are based in unconditional love and for the highest good of …. Those specific cords are to remain in place."

If you still believe that rituals and ceremonies are necessary when it comes to creating energy shifts then by all means continue with the ancient traditions. My personal preference is to go to the source – the power of word/thought! It's simple, straightforward, effective and immediate. All that's required is that you be clear as to your intention, and that may take some time to formulate. It has taken years for me to put into practice clear and concise wording that specifies my intention. The process has been one of gradual and steady improvement and enhanced clarity.

Unified Electrical Field

The cosmic energies continue to bombard Earth, supporting this shift in frequency to the higher vibratory levels. As mentioned in earlier chapters my non-physical friends were determined that in order I was able to understand their instruction and the general information they imparted simplicity of explanation was necessary. Given that generally I do not exhibit a strong scientific understanding of life, matter and the universe, to this day I'm deeply grateful for their basic descriptions and explanations. At one stage I clearly received information about the unified electrical field, which at that time was totally unfamiliar and new. This information was outlined in Chapter 1. The last point shared, "The human DNA contains the potential for enormous expansion. DNA has electrical force. Its expansion is activated by thought" is especially relevant and important.

It seems apparent that everything comes back to the power of thought/word! While I've briefly shared psychic insights about the likelihood of a unified energy field the reality is that there's still a great deal to be learned and understood about the vast cosmos and the role that humanity plays in the larger picture.

My contention has always been that the more you understand about the nature of creation, life purpose and the ways it's possible to maximize innate potential then the greater the ability for living meaningfully and achieving that particular purpose – whatever it may be. Gaining basic understanding of energy and its application to attaining greater fulfilment means the likelihood of enhanced ease in life. In other words, figure out where the flow is for you and follow it.

The two energy techniques shared below may offer you the potential for expanding your consciousness and enriching your life journey and the experiences that are on offer. Both are tried and tested techniques and have added value, in terms of heightened understanding and awareness for myself and clients alike.

Hemisphere Integration

As reiterated throughout my narrative, reducing mind chatter is critical to ultimately achieving the state where the voice of the soul becomes the expression of your consciousness. All practices such as breath work, meditation, communing with nature, opening your heart center, mindfulness of thought and speech are an integral component of deprogramming old thoughts and beliefs and reprogramming into a higher frequency. However, integration of right and left hemispheres is essential to the process. While the hemispheres are in a state of imbalance energetically there exists a tendency to rely on the old ways of thinking and functioning. With balanced energetic hemispheres there is greater ease in reprogramming both the conscious and subconscious minds, which in turn results in changes on every level in your life. These changes may be slight or subtle initially though eventually will have a far-reaching impact.

Not long ago science teaching indicated that the functioning of the brain was set and could not be changed, improved or modified in any way. The research in more recent years has clearly demonstrated that neuroplasticity of the brain is normal and innate. It is easy to regenerate neural pathways and to make new pathways depending on intention, thought and practice. This implies the fluidity and malleability aspects of the physical brain. It indicates that changes in thoughts and emotions result in neurological changes within the actual brain. This malleability and fluidity of the brain, I suspect, is a reason that energetic hemisphere integration is a plausible practice.

There exists an effective technique involving mind, intention and action for energetically integrating right and left hemispheres of the brain, which is described below. This is a procedure I happened to stumble upon many years ago. Unfortunately, I have no recollection of its actual source. I have found it to be highly effective and an easy practice to undertake. The practice does not take long and it's important to initially do it daily, then every few days, reduce it to weekly and from there on check in from time to time to see if an energy top-up is needed.

- Begin by being in a comfortable and relaxed seated position with feet flat on the ground and hands resting on your lap. Take slow, deep breaths and relax fully into feeling the breath in your body.
- This next step may sound slightly convoluted but once you get the hang of it you'll find it works effortlessly. Focus attention on the spot that sits mid-way between your coccyx and anus. That is the spot where you will begin building up energy. Begin by squeezing

the muscles in that region, as you do when undertaking Kegel pelvic floor muscle strengthening exercises.

- Squeeze repeatedly until you begin to feel an energy build up. Once there's plenty of energy in that area mentally say "Release and Fill" and feel the energy moving up your spinal cord (Kundalini pathway). It will immediately go to your energetic brain hemispheres.

- Most likely you'll initially feel an imbalance between your right and left hemispheres, one will be less full than the other. Keep repeating this process until you intuitively sense or know that both hemispheres are reasonably full and level.

- Once both are full mentally give the command "Integrate" and you should then sense or feel the energies swirling from one side to the other and back. If you are unable to feel or sense this happening then visualize or imagine it happening.

- Repeat the process, with the commands given, until you feel that both sides are as full as they possibly can be. Then quietly give gratitude for the process and the opportunity to now function with fully balanced and integrated hemispheres.

Remember to initially undertake this process daily, then every few days, once a week, once a month or as often as is needed. You'll find that gradually the hemispheres will hold the integration. Once this happens then other changes become apparent.

If you are a numbers person or someone who processes a lot of logical information it would not normally be easy to shift from that left brain functioning into the creative, intuitive right-side functioning. Creativity becomes so much easier with the energy brain integration and balancing. This enables easy shifting from being logical to applying intuition. The brain integration enables a greater ease and harmony when it comes to problem solving, resolution, decision making, and lateral thinking. It's like shifting from seeing the small picture only to seeing and knowing all sides of the bigger picture! Best of all you'll find an easy flow from being logical to creative back to being logical and so on. This actually saves time and energy on attempting to figure out things, as the brain integration enables you to access, with greater ease, so much more of what is already available to you but which you've previously been unable to retrieve.

You may feel uncertain or hesitant about undertaking this particular activity as it may appear unusual or for other reasons such as being concerned about its impact on your abilities and functioning. All I can say with certainty is that I've taught this activity in many classes and to numerous clients, in addition to undertaking this practice myself, and the results have always been positive.

The process of balancing and integrating right and left hemispheres needs to be completed and functioning fully before the next step, mind expansion, can be undertaken. This is an important point to be aware of. This energy change process is not like playing games of little or no consequence. Energy is energy. How it's used and applied can have highly uplifting consequences, or they can be less than desirable. When undertaking a new fitness regimen it's important to build up strength, flexibility and fitness gradually as this enables the body to build stamina and strength steadily. Running a marathon without a consistent training program can lead to serious physical health outcomes. It's the same when undertaking critical and intense energy changes. Making improvements sequentially is important, as this supports desired outcomes and prevents unintended consequences from occurring.

Mind Expansion

Over countless years my teachers in non-physical form have commented on the importance of using the mind for another of its intended purposes, which is mind expansion. When the mind continually processes conscious and subconscious chatter then it is fully occupied with minutiae. There is no room for anything else to occur. There is limited scope for change in perspective or understanding. Other writers have explored at length the complexity of the functioning of mind. Such writers include, but are not limited to Dr Charles Krebs, *A Revolutionary Way of Thinking,* and Torkom Saraydarian, *Thought and the Glory of Thinking.*

Overall my intention is to merely share information received from my teachers, while also acknowledging the value of other research that has been undertaken. While the information from my non-physical teachers is not scientifically, mathematically or biologically detailed it is nevertheless relevant and useful for those interested in exploring their higher potential. I also only ever share what I've experienced and often what has been shared with clients also.

As I understand it, the intended purpose for the mind is actually mind expansion. What is mind expansion and how can it be created? The mind was never intended to be a repository for storing mindless chatter and clutter. It was designed to be a powerful creator with unlimited potential. It is common for people to continually create their life through the energy of worry, regret, anxiety and fear. Conscious and subconscious thoughts create life. When both conscious and subconscious chatter are quietened then there exits infinite possibilities for expanded thinking and creation. In other words, nothing is impossible. There are no limits.

Powerful techniques for clearing the mind include regular meditation, breath work, martial arts practices and living in the moment. I keep reiterating this fact for good reason. Without consistent practice of some kind the mind tends to wander off on its own tangent, like an untrained canine companion. Dedication and commitment are essential for developing a state of being in the Now moment, free of thought and distracting emotions. Another essential and critical factor in preparing the mind for mind expansion is the need to have integration of right and left hemispheres of the brain as discussed above. Given our society's penchant for favouring left-brain thinking it is common for many people to have left brain dominance, with little functioning of their creative and intuitive right brain occurring.

In 1999 my non-physical teachers guided the following exercise. Prior to this I had the awareness that integration of right and left hemispheres of my brain had already commenced and was fully progressed. Little did I realize then the importance of the mind expansion technique and how my life would change as a consequence.

Mind Expansion Technique

In a meditation I was guided through a simple but powerful mind expansion process. Initially I was asked to focus on the area around the top of my head, but inside the skull. While this area consists of the brain it must be remembered that the physical brain connects with the mind and responds to information transmitted by the mind. Once my attention was focused I was asked to visualize a small box, shaped like a shoe box, sitting within the top part of my head. I visualized it as being a rich gold color. As I viewed it I noticed there was energy spinning outwards from the box shape. Gradually I was encouraged to observe it growing to the size of a basketball, all the while encompassing both hemispheres of the brain. Interestingly I observed that this was initially a rectangular shape, which with concentration gradually elongated into an elliptical form. I noticed that the shoe box structure gradually changed its shape, the more I concentrated. Also I gained the distinct impression that its round, elliptical form indicated its limitless potential for further expansion.

The now golden elliptical image continued slowly expanding. It moved beyond the top of my head slowly and steadily into a further expanded state. This continued outwards until it became apparent that this enlarged ellipse was fully connected to universal consciousness. It became indescribably massive in size and was still connected to my energy hologram at the same time. Eventually there were no lines constricting or limiting it in any way. This shape was very different to its initial shoebox shape; possibly indicating that being able to think outside the box was now a distinct reality. In fact, there was no box, there was simply a constant connection to the vast universal consciousness. There was no delineation or separation any more.

Realistically when reflecting about thinking outside the box I came to the conclusion that the box occupies only a very limited space in human awareness. The box contains memories, thoughts and emotions relating to all that has been known and experienced through one or more lifetimes. The box does not contain information outside those specifics. Therefore it is very limiting in its potential. It offers little opportunity for further growth, understanding and awareness of all that is. It prevents exploration of that vast unexplored universal consciousness of all thought, ideas and knowledge. Another way of expressing this is to ask, "What is inside the box?" The answer obviously is whatever you may know or have experienced. When you ask, "What is outside the box?" the answer is evident. It's everything else!

Mind expansion is a simple technique that enables you to leave the box mentality behind permanently and allows you instead limitless potential for growth and expansion. As I mentioned previously, these energy activities are to be undertaken mindfully and sequentially for optimal outcomes.

Later my non-physical friends communicated this message:

> "Imagine a tennis ball, watch it grow to the size of a basketball. That is the capacity of your mind, of the energy that you call your mind. All things are possible with thought. You can tele connect with others. You can split yourself into many and be in many places – different levels and times. All is multidimensional. You have the ability to transcend, to transmute and to create miracles with the energies. These energies are available to all, but not until they awaken. This is freedom. All have the ability to do this, but they must want it."

In another message I was reminded of the necessity of allowing the mind and imagination flexibility and always to use the energy and knowledge wisely. My teachers stressed that when exploring the potential of mind expansion the importance of always using energy for the highest good is paramount.

Remember that the mind is vast and limitless. When the clutter in both conscious and subconscious minds has been cleared and the soul becomes the voice of expression, then the mind can be used to create in new, exciting and unexplored ways. This creation ability goes beyond manifesting material possessions or lifestyle changes. It involves using the mind in a lateral way for a higher purpose. When doing this you are actually working with energy of a high vibration to create shifts, healing and new opportunities previously unexplored.

I strongly suggest that you not attempt the mind expansion exercise if you:

- are not fully comfortable and adept with meditation;
- are unsure if your energetic right and left hemispheres are integrated. This is where it's important to have undertaken that practice for some time;

- still hold unto fears about your spiritual path, or generally live a fear based life;
- still feel separate and disconnected from everyone and everything else;
- have unresolved issues that you are ignoring, suppressing or denying;
- do not regularly practice protection of your space, including physical body and energy hologram;
- are strongly inclined to be self-focused and coming from ego; and
- wish to use mind expansion for ulterior motives.

The power of thought and of the mind's vastness and potential cannot ever be underestimated or understated. One factor that limits your ability to tap into this wealth of potentiality is fear. This fear may be due to a host of reasons. Realistically, mind expansion should never be considered or attempted when fear is evident or sensed as residing on the subconscious level. When there is suspected fear present then its healing must be a priority.

Mind expansion is suitable and applicable for the individual who is fearless at the soul level, who has undergone regular and rigorous spiritual practice and is ready for this next step. If it were used for any purpose other than right reason, that individual would likely find him or herself in a spiritual quandary. The outcome would not be enlightening, and would most likely result in spiritual emergency.

Spiritual emergency is the term coined to explain overwhelming spiritual awakening. This is a sudden and powerful energetic opening, which may involve the precipitous development of psychic abilities, the ability to see non-physical entities, to predict events, and to generally have unintended access to the invisible layers that co-exist outside the normal co-created reality.

A spiritual emergency can be frightening and distressing. It is never to be taken lightly. Each spiritual emergency is unique to the individual undergoing the experience. At all times it is vitally important to maintain steady progress and learning in your journey into higher consciousness. This journey involves exploring and delving into territory that is unfamiliar and unknown and at all times caution is urged. It is only through a steady learning process that optimal understanding is possible. If, at any time, you feel a sense of fear or reluctance which may emanate from your body's response or inner knowing it's important to honour that response. Avoid taking your learning to new levels until you've mastered the earlier steps that gently lead you to feeling confident about energy engagement with experiences such as mind expansion.

What are the benefits of mind expansion? While this topic could be explored more extensively than I am covering at this stage, there are some advantages inherent in attaining this state. They include:

- being able to see the larger picture on a continual basis, while also understanding the smaller details;
- letting go of limiting perceptions and beliefs;
- working fully with all senses, including intuition;
- being able to explore limitless and exciting new possibilities;
- connecting with non-physical realities;
- increased ability to think laterally and creatively;
- using the mind to create and manifest in new ways for the betterment of all;
- exploring the untapped potential of the mind;
- experiencing an expanded sense of self, not in an egotistical way, but rather as the totality of all energy bodies within the hologram;
- discovering untapped skills and knowledge that previously were unavailable.

If you are tempted to explore mind expansion but are unsure of whether it is appropriate for your level of spiritual awareness I suggest that you allow some time to reflect on its possible merits as they relate to you. Meditation also assists in gaining clarity. Allowing yourself an opportunity to delve more deeply into what feels right enables you to step outside the normal routine of analytical assessment that is familiar to your mind. This is not a decision that can be lightly made. Give it serious consideration and reflection before deciding to proceed.

Moving Forward

As you are no doubt realizing there's a great deal more to this journey of consciousness awakening. You may refer to it as a spiritual journey or choose some other description to explain the process. Generally it's a steady progression, often requiring a lifetime of endeavour and commitment. Yet, with the cosmic energies so strong at this juncture in our history there's massive acceleration toward inner mastery and understanding.

In my first book, *Messages From Beyond*, containing channelled messages from the Arcturian Community there is a statement that baldly asserts the importance of the Now time you live in and the responsibility inherent in choosing to incarnate into this time of awakening. The message states:

> "We say again the answers are within you. It is you who must do the work in order to achieve this transformation. It is you who must make the shift from the thinking mode to the feeling mode. In doing this you will have mind expansion of undreamed proportions and you will know that the future of your planet and of coming generations is in your hands. It will not come outside of yourselves. We cannot stress this enough."

Chapter 10

Emotionally there have been many challenges and opportunities for great learning. Do not be alarmed by what you perceive to be non-attachment to anything in the physical dimension. This is an important aspect of awareness. Shifts in consciousness produce considerable changes in your physical reality.

There is significant difference between emotion and compassion. Emotion is a blessed condition of human embodiment, and the way your cultures experience physical existence is through the emotions. Unfortunately much of the human condition is tied into emotion that is conditional, and as such it is common for the emotions to rule your life while in physical embodiment. Understanding the nature of emotion is an essential component of the spiritual journey. In your situation you are not ruled by your emotions, you merely experience them and observe their impact and then you move forward. That is how the enlightenment process evolves – from having attachment to the emotion to eventually having no attachment. Having no attachment does not mean lacking compassion. Having greater spiritual alignment means shifting from having normal human emotions to coming to a state of unconditional compassion. Extending compassion to all and everything is a sign of emotional maturity.

Allow yourself to just be. In the being you will find the answers you seek. It is as simple as that. Be mindful of all that you do. Have conscious awareness around your thoughts and emotions. There are still some subtle reactions within you that will, in time, disperse. These are reflexive conditioning you have carried through, and which have been aggravated through your life dramas. Allow yourself to just be in each and every moment. While in a state of being pay attention to what you observe and feel. This will assist you greatly in understanding the nature of All That Is.

One more thing....be gentle with yourself. You exhibit considerable patience and acceptance in all situations. Yet, your desire to achieve your purpose, while commendable, can be lessened without reducing the outcomes that you seek. (Automatic writing, 2006)

The power of the mind cannot be underestimated or ignored. The reason I've devoted a substantial portion of my sharing to the exploration of its integral role in reality creation is to reinforce its important role and function in your life. Hopefully in doing so you are gaining greater respect and understanding of its overall versatility. You are the creator of all that you've experienced and are the ongoing creator of whatever is still to transpire. Conscious creation is your responsibility.

This does not mean that you are able to avoid negative situations or that you can use your mind to completely override any challenges you may confront in your life journey. There are reasons for this and they are valid. The reasons relate to the innate wisdom of your higher non-physical aspect. This is sometimes referred to as soul, spirit or higher self. At times the conscious mind (ego) is determined that a specific outcome will be achieved. When your soul needs to fulfil a challenging experience it will do so, irrespective of your ego wishes.

It is easy to assume that mind is the only determinant of your fates. An individual whose life is dominated by the mind tends to view the world largely through the mental level of the energy hologram. The automatic writing message above refers to the role of human emotions. For some individuals emotions are often used as being the determinant of how life is viewed and experienced. An over focus on either the mind or the emotions may lead to an overall imbalance in the energy hologram. An emphasis on one results in the other being either overlooked or ignored altogether. Here I'm simplifying something that energetically is actually far more complex in order to emphasize the fact that ultimately imbalance is counterproductive to the energy hologram, and therefore also to the physical body.

In order to maximize the potential of the mind a vital aspect of functioning needs to be involved and integrated. This is the functioning of the heart center. According to studies undertaken it's been determined that conscious awareness does not originate in the brain/mind only. Apparently consciousness emerges when the body and mind interact, with the heart center playing an important and pivotal role in the process.

Heart Consciousness

The heart, which is a highly complex system, seemingly has its own functional brain hub. It communicates information to the brain and throughout the body via electromagnetic field fluctuations and interactions. The electrical component of the heart's field is about sixty times greater than that produced by the actual brain. It's so powerful that it permeates every cell, atom and molecule in the body. It does this by pulsing waves of electromagnetic energy that radiates out from the heart and from there interacts with organs and all body systems.

It's been found that emotional states affect the heart and its overall functioning. When you live with mainly high frequency emotions on a regular basis there is a noticeable and distinctive manner of heart performance. This has been shown to increase awareness of, and sensitivity to others. I would postulate that a mind diet of low frequency emotions has the potential to ultimately result in physical weakening of the heart, and therefore the cardiovascular and possibly other interconnected body systems.

A vast amount of research has been undertaken by the HeartMath Institute Research Center for more than twenty-eight years. (www. heartmath.org) Researchers at the center have explored the "physiological mechanisms by which the heart and brain communicate and how the activity of the heart influences…. perceptions, emotions, intuition and health". According to their ongoing research over the years it was the "heart rate variability, or heart rhythms that stood out as the most dynamic and reflective indicator of one's emotional states, and therefore, current stress and cognitive processes". This led to deeper exploration and understanding of communication pathways and patterns between the heart and brain. According to their research findings it "appeared that the heart could affect…awareness, perceptions and intelligence". Ultimately studies since then have indicated that "heart coherence is an optimal physiological state associated with increased cognitive function, self-regulatory capacity, emotional stability and resilience".

Some other points relating to the heart having its own brain and consciousness include, though may not necessarily be limited to:

- Consciousness emerges from the brain and body acting together;
- The heart is now acknowledged as a complex system containing its own functional brain;
- It is a sensory organ, a sophisticated center for receiving and processing information;
- The nervous system within the heart enables it to learn, remember and make function decisions that are independent of the brain's cerebral cortex;
- Emotional states impact heart functioning. Sustained positive emotions give rise to a distinct code of functioning, called "psychophysiological coherence", which basically increases awareness and consciousness; and
- The heart's electromagnetic field is highly likely to be involved in intuitive perception.

Biologically the heart is considered by medical science to be a pump. Its role is to pump and circulate blood. Via this process it also supports the circulation of the lymph. According to the HeartMath Institute the heart is a "highly complex information-processing center with its own functional brain, commonly called the *heart brain* that communicates with and influences the cranial brain via the nervous system, hormonal system and other pathways".

The HeartMath Institute has developed techniques to enhance personal coherence in mental functioning, health and wellbeing, perception, energy levels and happiness. It's been demonstrated that practicing those techniques has increased heart coherence and other positive outcomes, including feeling more balanced and healthier. If you are feeling unsure about how to shift from mind/emotion dominance to heart centered functioning you may find it worthwhile doing some reading on the HeartMath Institute website.

Shifting to Heart Centered Consciousness

In life you think and direct energy to where you aspire or intend to be. For example, once there is awareness of the importance of living in the moment then you continually make reference to this. Your language reinforces the fact that you live in the moment. Over time there is a repetition of that energy which builds up so that instead of merely repeating the same words you actually step into the feeling state of living in the moment.

The point I'm making is that talking about something is different to feeling it. Yet, in order to step into the feeling state there has to be plenty of talking and even visualizing, which then builds up an energy momentum and ultimately leads up to the shift of experiencing the feeling state. Once fully immersed in that feeling state it's virtually impossible to revert back to just talking about a conceptual experience. The concept actually becomes the experience. I view this feeling state as a vibratory state, as there's been a slight shift in vibration due to the constant repetition. This is a clear example of energy amplification in action. As you attain that feeling vibratory state there is a subtle shift within your energy hologram and consciousness.

It is the same with shifting to a state of living with heart centered consciousness. Lots of talk and action precede the feeling state. Once in the heart feeling state there is a huge shift on all levels – physically, mentally, emotionally, energetically and spiritually. Being in a feeling state of functioning through the heart center ultimately means there's no need to constantly engage in thoughts or to even express words. The energy of being in that state takes precedence and anything that does not resonate with this new state of being feels incredibly uncomfortable, as it lacks harmony.

Shifting to heart centered consciousness, however, cannot occur until a great deal of inner work has taken place. This involves healing on all levels in relation to self and others. In the sessions I conduct I'm emphatic that the energy memories based in the lower three chakras require a lot of clearing and healing. When working solely on shifting to heart centered consciousness without doing the inner work the result will end up being out of balance. The fear and trauma pain triggers that sit deep within will always manifest, like a virus in a computer, resulting in dissonance and possibly even considerable pain.

Heart Centered Techniques

How do you shift from mind/emotion centered functioning to heart centered functioning? This requires a massive change in reality creation. Yet, taking it steadily means that eventually great strides are made in this process. While I'm not suggesting that mind/emotion centered dominance can be solely attributed to ego based functioning, my experience shows that often there's a correlation or connection between the two.

If you feel that you may be more focused on operating from a mind/emotion perspective and are feeling that a change is needed then there are some basic techniques that can be applied in everyday situations. They include:

- Giving gratitude daily, as many times as you have the opportunity. This is an ongoing process and though what you express gratitude for may change the act of giving gratitude needs to be as ingrained as the act of breathing. When in a true state of living with heart centered consciousness the expression of gratitude and appreciation does not require thought. It becomes a feeling state and joyful experience.
- Living in the moment. Find the technique that works for you. My personal preference is the breathing technique referred to earlier. Feedback from other people has confirmed the high degree of efficacy of breath work in creating the energy of the Now moment.
- Express love daily, and constantly. Whether it be to nature, body, health, friends, family and so on. Expressions of love, whether they be verbal, physical, mental or emotional go a long way to creating that feeling state.
- Apply forgiveness to self and others whenever a situation arises that brings up painful memories. Rather than dwelling on the issue or emotion, mentally affirming, "I love myself, I forgive myself" is extremely powerful in shifting the pain energy. This can also

include an additional statement, "I love…., I forgive…." when in relation to others.

- Do what you enjoy and gives pleasure. The more you do the things that enthuse and inspire you the greater the reduction of inner stress.

- Let go of toxic situations and people. Sometimes it's not possible to do this so instead I suggest that letting go of the anxiety and stress reduces the level of inner tension. My favourite mantras in this regard are, "This too shall pass" and "It is what it is". This in no way diminishes the nature of the issue or situation. Instead it creates an energetic barrier, distancing you from the situation and allowing greater ease within.

- Let go of your story. Most people carry memories of experiences that have been painful. Continually talking about those experiences, remembering them, re-visiting the emotions keeps them truly alive and feeds an energy trigger that doesn't abate. I'm not saying ignore or suppress the emotions. Instead, when they surface I've found the statement beginning with, "I release with love….." to be highly effective in reducing any stored pain memory. Sometimes that statement needs to be repeated countless times, along with doing forgiveness work, but ultimately it's well worth the time and energy.

The eventual outcomes of applying these techniques is a shift from mind/emotion centered functioning to a heart centered consciousness, which in turn results in tremendous enrichment of all life experiences.

Learning Self Love

I am emphatic when I say that unconditional, universal love is impossible to manifest and hold constantly until you hold the vibration and feeling of self-love. This statement may sound harsh. It's not intended that way. It's merely a bald statement of fact. The more you engage in activities to open yourself to be fully heart centered the greater the outcomes. There will be moments when you will feel as if you've arrived, that you are truly living with unconditional love. Those moments are the practice moments, the ones that provide a hint of what is to come. Eventually it's possible to sustain the frequency of unconditional love. It requires a lot of practice and a belief in yourself that you can achieve this goal.

In western culture you are conditioned and encouraged to put the needs of others ahead of your own. You are taught via language that when you behave in certain ways then you're worthwhile as an individual. Also the opposite occurs when you are condemned for your actions, for that is when love and approval are withheld. From an early age you are told that "you're a good girl or boy" when your words and actions are pleasing to others. In much the same way approval is withheld when you displease your parents, friends, other adults, religious teachings and so on. This kind of love is conditional. It is dispensed when you please another person or fall into line with societal beliefs and mores. Conditional love has strings attached, and to my way of thinking is extremely unhealthy for your psyche.

The impact of conditional love is exhibited in countless ways within our culture. Feelings of inadequacy, lack of self-worth, low self-esteem, and so on are prevalent within our co-created reality. Social media also contributes to the creation of not being enough, which greatly impacts the confidence and self-esteem of countless individuals.

Unconditional love is the opposite of conditional love. You accept and love yourself as you are – weaknesses, flaws, imperfections as well as talents, differences, quirks and idiosyncrasies. In most instances what is required is a complete reprogramming of self-talk and actions in order to attain a state of unconditional love. Given the quality of the research undertaken by the HeartMath Institute it's well worth undergoing a transformation into heart centered unconditional love. The physical, mental, emotional and spiritual benefits are well demonstrated in their ground breaking research, which has been undertaken over a period of nearly three decades.

In computer language, input equals output. When you input love affirming words and actions into your energy hologram then the energy hologram emits the frequency of love. In other words, you create and manifest that unconditional love. The energy hologram recognizes the frequency and vibration of love and thrives on it. The finely tuned subatomic grid structure responds positively. The sensitive microscopic thread-like strands of the matrix regain their strength, flexibility and balance. The nourishment received from expressions of self-love and self-acceptance gradually releases stored emotions, fears, beliefs and perceptions. The energy of self-love replaces whatever has been released (from the conscious and subconscious minds), and provides further sustenance to the grid structured hologram.

Coming to a state of complete self-acceptance and self-love involves continual awareness of thoughts and behaviours, and replacing negative perceptions with the energy of love. It is an ongoing process. There will also be changes within your physical reality. Like attracts like, so you will attract people and situations with similar vibrational frequencies, resulting in new harmonious friendships and relationships. Similarly, you will attract fewer negative issues and experiences into your life. You will find, however, that separation occurs from those whose negative energies do not align with your new frequencies. I refer to this aspect as frequency dissonance. Accept this process of change and release with love those relationships that do not come from a place of unconditional love.

Creating Self Love

Coming to a state of self-love releases you from the need for external validation. This is because you've reached a space where you know yourself and happily allow your instinctual knowing to guide you. The extent to which you are able to attain a state of self-love depends on your determination and also the amount of inner work you undertake. As mentioned previously, if your current life is relatively pain and trauma free and your other lifetimes are similarly inclined then the breadth and scope of inner work required will most likely seem slight. Others who, at the soul level have chosen lifetimes of struggle and hardship may find the process daunting and seemingly never-ending. As with the suggestions below, be mindful that change is a process. Be patient with yourself and have no expectations as to outcomes. Instead, notice and enjoy the subtle changes as they occur.

Some suggestions for constructively creating heart centered functioning include:

- Speaking and thinking positively about yourself. Denigration, self-deprecation and sarcasm can be eliminated with practice.

- Monitoring and assessing the thoughts and beliefs you hold about yourself. When a negative thought surfaces replace it immediately with a positive, loving and nurturing thought and image. Remember the subconscious is literal; whatever you visualize becomes imprinted.
- The more these two steps are practiced, the stronger the feelings of self-acceptance and love become. When you fill your energy hologram with loving and appreciative thoughts about you there is less opportunity for the negative perceptions to dominate.
- Continue expressing feelings of self-love, even when it feels pointless and ridiculous. The barrage of positive thoughts and words holds frequency. Their impact on the subconscious and physical body, while subtle, ultimately has the power to change your life.
- Ensure thoughts, emotions, words and actions are in alignment in order to achieve the greatest energy shift. The more you focus intention in this regard the greater the shift.
- Speak your mind. Ensure you honor what feels right for you. This does not mean there is license to speak derogatorily or aggressively. At all times honor others as you too would like to be respected and honoured.
- A well-known daily practice that actually works though may seem daunting initially, is to look closely into a mirror, preferably first thing in the morning. Look into your eyes and say, "I love me, I love you". Hold your gaze steady for as long as possible, and truly see the inner beauty you hold.
- Be aware of the emotions you hold as you undertake self-love strategies. Do your emotions match your intentions? It may be that you would benefit from doing some forgiveness work on yourself. Or, possibly additional gratitude could be given to your body.
- At every opportunity ask, "How do I feel?" This enables you to connect with the feelings you hold in your heart center. It assists you to transcend a natural tendency to focus from the mental/emotional and ego perspective.
- Be clear about your boundaries. Use the word "no" as often as you feel the need, instead of acquiescing to the wishes and demands of

others. Make it your favourite word for a month and gauge how often you normally would have responded "yes" instead. People pleasing does not support the process of embracing self-love.

- Give to others when you feel inclined, not when it's expected of you. Sometimes an unexpected compliment can make a real difference in someone else's life. The act of giving unselfishly is enriching. It creates feelings of inner worth and warmth.
- Undertake activities that nurture and nourish your spirit. Anything that lifts your feeling of worthiness enriches the vibration of self-love.
- In meditation visualize your heart center as being filled with the frequency of love. In your mind's eye begin to slowly expand the love from your heart to the rest of your body. Visualize it as a color that feels right for you – it may be gold, pink, purple, green – whatever you feel your body needs at that particular time. Doing this on a regular basis has an effect on the energy hologram, and that gradually reaches your physical body, supporting all your body's systems and organs.
- Walk barefoot and spend time in nature on a regular basis. Connecting with nature reduces stress in addition to providing healing to the energy hologram.
- Undertake healing work on feelings of grief, betrayal, being broken-hearted and any other emotional trauma that may prevent you from fully giving and receiving love.

As the process of creating an inner landscape based on self-love and valuing progresses, the frequency of compassion slowly emerges. Compassion is a state of accepting everything and everyone as they are. It's based on understanding the nature of reality, co-creation and accepting the limitations of the world as it exists. However, generally once the state of compassion is gained you then live your truth, your inner core knowing that everything else is simply the stage where the life dramas are played out.

One of the significant benefits of living with unconditional love is that it holds a vibration with a high frequency. It is soft and gentle, yet is also extremely powerful. Simply being in a space of compassion and unconditional love has the power to change everything. It may change relationships, friendships and life situations and circumstances. As well, you generate an energy that also benefits nature, all that you connect with and also Mother Earth. In my opinion, unconditional love is the most powerful change agent available to humanity. Change your frequency, change your life.

Indicators of Compassionate Unconditional Love

How can you measure your level of success in achieving a state of compassionate unconditional love? It is possible to roughly determine whether a state of self-love and acceptance has been genuinely integrated and established. In the book *Inner Adventures*, Colin P. Sisson described a bill of rights for self-lovers, which seems to sum up the gist of what self-love is about. The points listed below are worthy of aspiring to. You may even reflect on whether you have achieved this state of self-love and acceptance. Or, the list may be used as a guide for improvement or making changes you may deem necessary. The qualities listed in the bill of rights for self-lovers are:

- As a self-lover it is perfectly acceptable to be as I choose to be. This means shifting from conditional love functioning into self-honoring.
- I have the right to think and feel as I choose. While this sounds straight forward it's actually more complicated. How much of what you think and feel has been conditioned since childhood? How much is the result of peer pressure or societal expectations?
- I am the ultimate judge of my own actions and am responsible for them. This does not mean self-criticism or flagellation. It relates to being able to compassionately assess your actions and determining where change or improvement could be made.
- I have the right and freedom to choose who I love and to allow myself to be loved in return.
- I love and respect myself. Again, peer pressure and societal expectations may play a subconscious role in this regard. Letting them go is often a major challenge.
- I am able to change, grow, learn and make mistakes.

- I am responsible for all my actions and thoughts/emotions.
- I am able to say "no" without needing the approval of other people.
- My privacy and time alone are important, and I honor that.
- I have the right to ask questions and to expect reasonable answers on all matters affecting my life.
- I am trustworthy. Because of this I expect that I will be treated as such.
- If I make a mistake it is my responsibility to correct it to the best of my ability.
- My decisions are my responsibility. It is unnecessary to make excuses, give explanations or justifications.
- It is my responsibility to ensure I have integrity in all actions without affecting other people adversely. This involves sensitivity to and mindfulness of other people's needs, ideology, perceptions and so on.
- I am responsible for solving my problems, for making decisions and for creating my own happiness. In other words, my happiness does not rely or depend on anyone else. My happiness is an inner feeling that comes from compassion and unconditional love.

Fully living a state of heart centered consciousness also results in other changes. The desire to judge or criticize completely dissipates. This is due to the fact that you no longer judge yourself. You accept yourself as you are. Therefore you simply see others as they are without being critical. Actually you come to see the beauty in life, instead of the harshness. The desire or need for conflict also disappears. Conflict signifies the polarities existing in the world, and that energy now lacks resonance when living from the heart.

In order to know and feel unconditional heart centered love it has to be experienced within, as well as extended to others. Living from the heart center involves bringing compassion, tolerance, acceptance and empathy to every situation. It means relegating the intellect and emotions to the back seat, and allowing the heart feeling state to predominate in all life situations.

Symptoms of Change

Attaining a state of unconditional heart centered love frequency involves quite a journey. It is a process fraught with change, unexpectedness, discomfort and even pain. It involves letting go of old energy (beliefs, programs and so on) and gradually embracing new opportunities and perspectives. You are shifting from lower density frequency to higher density frequency. The changes in your energy hologram are enormous, which is why a step-by-step process takes place.

Over the years I've heard individuals aspiring to become fully spiritually evolved lament the fact that, as yet, they are unable to bi-locate or time travel or generally undertake the magical manifestations of sages and gurus of ancient traditions. All the meditations and other spiritual practices support and further the possibility of energy manipulation, of that there is no doubt. Regardless of aspirations held by any individual the deeper inner work must be undertaken to attain the status and skills of the mystics. It is a never ending process. The magic of the aspirations is that along the way there is scope for dramatic change in life circumstance. Life can be sweeter. It can and does become easier as your frequency shifts to higher levels.

Some of the symptoms, or indications, of change occurring in your energy hologram include:

- Body aches and pains. These are often evident in the back, neck and shoulders and any other part of your body that holds energy imprints. Changes in DNA expansion contribute to this happening. Your body releases blocked energy, as well as cellular and energetic memory from all times.
- Disrupted and unusual sleep patterns. You may have intense, even disturbing dreams for a period of time. The subconscious is undergoing a process of healing and releasing. Dreams are the vehicle for that profound process.
- Periods of deep sleep. This is the body's way of integrating and processing the energetic changes. Deep sleep, inertia and periods of unusual lethargy are often symptomatic of the changes. They do pass; it's a stage of the energy shift process.

- Sensitivity to denser foods. As your body shifts to the higher vibration it requires organic, light foods. You may even experience a loss of appetite. There may be times when you crave specific foods or even feel the need to eat more frequently. You may change to a plant based food lifestyle. Denser foods (processed, refined and fake foods) hold an energy that does not resonate with the higher frequency changes occurring within your hologram.

- Heightened sensitivity to surroundings, including people, noise and other stimulation. This often results in feelings of being overwhelmed.

- Loss of balance, dizziness, ringing in ears, sore eyes, insomnia, headaches, heart palpitations and difficulty in breathing deeply. These are all transient symptoms. My personal experience has been that they're all energetic and not physical in origin. This is due to the energetic frequency shifts occurring.

- Lack of tolerance for lower vibrational things and activities. This involves letting go of some old habits and instead opting for new opportunities.

- Intense body heat, including night sweats and hot flashes. These indicate your body is burning up cellular memory.

- Heightened sensitivity and reactivity to lunar cycles and other cosmic configurations.

On an emotional level there may be varying reactions within. You may feel deep inner sadness for no apparent reason. There may be emotional pain from this and other times releasing, which does not resonate with the new, higher vibrational frequencies. You may feel a loss of passion or desire to create. There may be feelings of loneliness and aloneness. You may experience intensified emotions such as anxiety, panic, hysteria and depression. These intense emotions indicate that deep unresolved fears are surfacing and are ready to be released. Their vibration does not harmonize with the new frequencies you are creating.

On a mental level there may be feelings of disorientation or an inability to string together coherent thoughts. There may be periods of intense stress, which is due to your body's response to the higher frequencies. Your energy hologram undergoes a process of releasing all that is within and holds a lower vibration. This results in stress, discomfort and pain on every level. There may be some memory loss, which I learned from my memory erasure incident is simply your energy consciousness releasing extraneous memory. Temporary memory loss is not to be confused with dementia onset.

Spiritually there are also changes, some more evident than others depending on your individual circumstance. You may feel disoriented, ungrounded and unconnected. You may even find yourself shifting out of different realities and dimensions. There may be a strong yearning to go "home", with "home" being somewhere else, out in the great cosmos. You may access other dimensions and realities, which means opening the doors to latent psychic abilities. You may lose your sense of self, which is much like a snake shedding its skin. Your awareness and understanding of universal truths may undergo a major shift.

Most likely you have experienced some or many of these symptoms and shifts at some stage. They are largely energetic in nature though are often questioned as being physical in origin. Generally I've learned that the symptoms move around in my body, from one place to the next to the next. They vary in intensity and then fade. After that I sense a new lightness within, there's more energy and my thinking feels clearer. However, my suggestion to anyone who experiences any of the symptoms mentioned is to seek medical advice if the symptoms persist and worsen. Differentiating between energetic shifts and physical conditions can be tricky. It takes time and practice to fully know and understand your own body. This is why it's important to practice self-love, as self-love is a critical aspect to knowing yourself fully on all levels.

Chapter 11

I sat down to meditate and almost immediately went in deep. My mind was totally relaxed and empty, could feel the silence within and without. It was during this time that I began to experiment with the Theta healing, though am not sure how effective my endeavours are to date. Then I felt the presence of Zachary (my guide at that time) and he discoursed for quite a while. Seems Theta healing is extremely powerful. Zachary also talked about my current life. Seems that I have not yet commenced my real life purpose.

Listening to Zachary was like listening to soothing music. His words came and went and in time I was back into the stillness. My whole body felt cocooned within it, totally relaxed and not desiring any movement or change, enjoying the sensations while they lasted. Gradually I became aware of another energy right next to me. Slowly I assessed its source and it was very much from the Light. I instinctively knew the importance of remaining completely still. On another level I was keen to ascertain exactly what was happening and so tuned in to the energy mass that was coming into the left side of my body.

I maintained the stillness, breathing slowly and almost imperceptibly. The strength and intensity of the energy mass deepened. I felt it gradually merging into my energy field. At times it felt extremely hot and even slightly uncomfortable. Yet I remained still, knowing that movement would interfere with the process. The greatest discomfort was experienced when the merging and integration occurred in my lower legs. The heat was searing and intense. Finally, the process was complete. Yet, I remained still for some time. It felt right to do this, maybe to allow time for full integration and some settling in phase. When I came out of my meditative state I knew that something extremely significant had occurred. I felt extremely relaxed and uplifted by the experience, and knew that another energy had integrated into mine for a higher purpose.

Immediately upon coming back into a fully aware state I began to check my perceptions by using the pendulum. When using this dowsing instrument it is often as if I already know the answers before I even begin to ask the questions. The pendulum is a means of verifying my thoughts. Instinctively I knew that the energy mass that had integrated was from an Ascended Master, and when I asked the pendulum received a strong "yes" in response. I didn't even have to ask who, as I knew intuitively it was Kuthumi. I also heard his name in my head simultaneously. My overwhelming reaction was one of feeling blessed, humbled and loved. There was no buzz in my mind around why, what for, etc. On another level I graciously accepted the initiation or blessing and understood that all would be revealed in time.

A tingling sensation coursed through my body for the remainder of the day. I felt as though I was vibrating at a higher level – and it felt good! Kuthumi is a teacher and I feel that his teachings will come through me. Also feel this integration is another step in the process of preparing me for what lies ahead. (Journal entry, 2005)

My reasoning for choosing the journal entry above, from 2005, for this chapter is straightforward. In everyday life focus tends, mainly, to be on the practical mental, emotional and physical needs and aspirations. These are essential for wellbeing and it's easy to assume that consciously those needs can be met through hard work, diligence and application. In my experience there is a great deal of support from the non-physical reality, which has the potential to accelerate individual growth, understanding and expansion. This is available for everyone once there is recognition of its vital role in enhancing life's challenges and processes. It's this recognition and acceptance that can hasten, or fast-track, your awareness into expanded consciousness. In other words, you don't have to feel alone on this journey called life. There is amazing energy support from benevolent non-physical beings who encourage and assist in ways that are unimaginable to the average conscious human mind.

My experience of having this particular energy integration was one of numerous that have occurred over a period spanning nearly thirty years. Each time the experience is different, as is the knowledge and understanding of its purpose. Have they made life easier? Have they lightened the load? I am unable to answer that categorically. What I do know, however, is that knowing there's support from the non-physical beings, our space brothers and sisters, is reassuring. I also know that my life would not be the same if this ongoing support, combined with energy upgrades and integration, had not occurred. It would otherwise have been more difficult to wade through life's problems and issues, with its many ups and downs. This non-physical energy has provided support, comfort and reassurance during the darkest of times in a way that nothing else could have done. Many a time I have sought clarification and explanation as to the why of an issue or situation. It has always been given with love and compassion, thereby reducing my stress levels. I've learned that all I need do is ask. Just as that's all you need to do. Once that's done then the responsibility for listening and heeding the guidance becomes the next step in life's journey.

As an aside, there have been times when I've questioned and even doubted this non-physical guidance only to eventually realize that it's been perfect every time. There is no doubt that I signed up for these experiences prior to incarnating into this body. It's not what everyone would experience, or choose to experience, at the soul level. However, no matter your soul direction and choices there is still scope for you to receive guidance and support from the non-physical realms to some degree. At the very least it's highly reassuring to know that there is more to life and the universe than life in just this one particular time experience.

Maslow's Hierarchy of Needs

At the end of Chapter Seven I very briefly alluded to Maslow's Hierarchy of Needs. This is a psychological profile of basic human needs and their importance to the process of self-actualization. It's important to discuss the relevance of the hierarchy of needs, including the process of self-actualization, especially as to how it relates to energy, frequency and vibration. Mahatma Gandhi is reported to have said that there are many roads to the One. I take this to mean that there are different ways of making sense of life and the universe, and that there's no one ideology that is suitable for everyone. In this chapter my focus is on Maslow's

Hierarchy of Needs while endeavouring to link it with spirituality and quantum consciousness. You may find greater resonance with the concept and explanation of self-actualization or it may be a more suitable context for understanding the relationship between spirituality and quantum consciousness.

What is self-actualization and how is it attained? Why is it relevant? Embarking upon the road less travelled, which is another way of describing the journey into higher consciousness, is fraught with uncertainty, twists and turns. Understanding Maslow's hierarchy of needs may help you feel more comfortable and certain of your particular passage through life, just as it may help you see another perspective on all that I have shared on energy and its complexity.

According to Wikipedia in 1943 Abraham Maslow submitted a paper entitled "A Theory of Human Motivation", which was published in *Psychological Review*. This theory, or model, seeks to explain human motivation and growth based on needs that drive everyday functioning and existence. His focus was to pinpoint the phases or stages of need that ultimately would lead to a point of authentic growth in an individual. And, ultimately isn't that a worthy aspiration, one that many people strive to attain? Maslow argued that motivation to achieve certain needs is instinctive, and that some needs take precedence over others. The original five hierarchies of needs are described below. Maslow posited that once a level of need is met then the next level up drives motivation. In other words, there are stages, or levels, of attainment needed prior to an individual becoming fully self-actualized. The levels are:

1. Physiological needs. These are the needs for basic survival including food, water, clothing, shelter, sex, sleep, and so on.
2. Safety needs. This includes security, protection, stability, freedom, and more.
3. Belonging needs. This includes love, social integration, interpersonal relationships and similar aspects of human connection. This stage only emerges when the previous two levels are fulfilled.
4. Esteem needs. Maslow defined two components to this level. The first being self-esteem, including dignity, independence, mastery

and achievement. The second aspect of this relates to the desire for good or solid reputation or respect from others.

5. Self-actualization needs. This involves realizing personal potential, seeking personal growth and self-fulfilment.

These needs were diagrammatically demonstrated in a pyramid format with physiological needs being at the base and taking up the largest space. Each need thereafter sat above the base and was represented as a smaller portion of the overall needs. It immediately becomes apparent, when viewing the needs represented in pyramid format that the first four needs take precedence before self-actualization even becomes possible. Without the previous four levels being fulfilled it's difficult, if not downright impossible, to become a fully self-actualized individual.

My understanding of this model of human motivation is that self-actualization is a goal worth working toward. It ultimately is the level where full understanding of who you are and why you're here on the planet is attained. It's where you become fully authentic, living with integrity and I'd even go so far as to say that you could possibly be living an aware and enlightened existence. It's a space of calm, non-judgment, compassion and love where you transcend most of the foibles of the human condition. This, in no way means that sainthood is about to be bestowed. Rather it indicates that you've largely left behind the pettiness, uncertainty, judgments and insecurities of life because you now know who you are, weaknesses and strengths alike. Because of this knowledge you recognize that you are powerful and humbled simultaneously. You also know that life in the mortal world is an illusion. This you know this with every cell of your being and not as an intellectual knowing.

Indicators of Self Actualization

Apparently self-actualization occurs when you're able to reach your full potential – whatever that may be or may mean. However, it seems it's uncommon for individuals to actually achieve a state of self-actualization. In most instances it's considered the exception, rather than the norm, according to the experts in the field. Still, it's worth considering as a goal, one to be striving for in the long term. Over the course of a lifetime there are plentiful opportunities for ongoing growth in understanding and awareness. There actually is no pinnacle to be reached. My non-physical friends often mention the word "refinement", indicating that the opportunity exists to become better skilled and adept at whatever is undertaken. The aim is to refine and improve continually. As this occurs there's scope for enhancement of whatever skills, knowledge, behaviours and awareness that already exist. Even a "master" has the potential to continue learning and refining their understanding. So, there's no defining end to this process. Becoming self-actualized is simply another step in the process of human evolution, one that is available to everyone.

Apparently Maslow studied the characteristics of individuals he believed or deemed to be self-actualized. Some of the more evident characteristics include, though are not limited to:

- Willingness to embrace the unknown and the ambiguous. Some well-known historical individuals such as Albert Einstein and Abraham Lincoln may have displayed this tendency.
- Self-acceptance of self, including flaws and imperfections. This views shortcomings as personal traits, and not necessarily something that needs modification or correction.
- Enjoying the journey and not necessarily focusing on the destination. This tendency affords the opportunity to fully embrace all available possibilities and aspects of life, not just the successes.
- Being unconventional though without the desire to flaunt a lack of convention. Self-actualized individuals recognize that others would not understand or even accept their unconventionality.
- Motivated by the desire and intention to undertake personal growth on a continual basis. This involves the development of self, and not the fulfilment or gratification of self.
- They recognize there is a purpose or mission in life. In most instances this purpose or mission is selfless and is often humanitarian based.
- Small things are of little or no consequence. Issues are universal, not local. Focus is on the big picture and not the minutiae.
- Living with an attitude of gratitude and deep, constant appreciation.

- Relationships are deep though with few people while simultaneously identifying and holding affection for humanity as a whole.
- They are humble because they are aware and understand just how little they actually know.
- They resist enculturation, meaning they see beyond the beliefs and values readily accepted by wider society. They make up their own minds and decisions despite what the majority may adhere to. Their codes of ethics are autonomous, and are not dictated to by society.
- They also have their foibles, weaknesses and imperfections. But, then, no-one is perfect because perfection is an ideal, not a reality. Being human entails the whole gamut of emotions and beliefs. Most of which at some stage surface and provide an opportunity for further growth in understanding and behaviours.

The descriptions of these traits and tendencies was found at www.huffpost. com/entry/maslow-the-12-characteris b 7836836

Growth Process

While it's possible to aspire to a state and space of self-actualization (enlightenment) it truly is a steady and generally slow process. In many instances, although not exclusively, it becomes more evident with maturity. Maturity is not necessarily the gaining of years; it's frequently attained through life experiences. Often it's the toughest times in life that accelerate the deeper knowing and awareness within. Yet self-actualization can never be fully attained without achieving and fulfilling the first four needs of the hierarchy. There is a sequence to the process that is essential to achieving the final state of awareness.

Let's be realistic. Maslow described a hierarchy of needs, the basis of which reflected his findings and research into the human psyche last century. It is a guideline which provides insight and even offers an explanation for human potential. Regardless, his work has been greatly admired, quoted, researched and even modified since it was published in 1943. Therefore it can be surmised that there is validity and applicability to his research, given the interest and research in the field that continues to this day. In order to achieve a higher state of awareness there is a process of specific needs and growth that have to be met before you ultimately reach a level of self-actualization.

The first four needs are largely linked to physical, mental and emotional aspects of life. Where there is a level of fulfilment an individual then is able to explore further the meaning and purpose of life. Some individuals would view this as being spiritual, others would simply view it as feeling fulfilled. It is all a matter of perception.

In the book *Ask And It Is Given* by Esther and Jerry Hicks there is a classic example given of how the growth and change process operates. Esther channels a non-physical group called Abraham. Wisdom is dispensed sagely along with advice and suggestions as to how to create change and growth, based on the Law of Attraction. Abraham stated that in order to gain your desires your vibration must match the vibration of whatever it is that you are seeking. It was then explained that the process of change is gradual and steady. The emotional scale was used as a clear and concise example of how this process works.

Abraham listed a whole range of emotions with depression/grief as having the lowest frequency and with bliss/love being the highest. Between those emotions at the extremes there were many others listed. It was indicated that it's not possible to shift from depression to bliss – in terms of frequency – immediately or even overnight. To be in a state of bliss, love or joy and to be in it constantly requires moving up the scale of emotions, one step at a time. This progression involves a great deal of inner work, including letting go and undertaking new practices. These new practices, whether they be affirmations, changing self-talk and so on are the process by which change and growth occur.

In other words, it's impossible to move directly from A to Z. The process involves moving from A to B to C and onwards due to the learning that is gained with each step taken. It's the same with the Maslow Hierarchy. Self-actualization is a process and from my understanding there is never an ending to that progression. The refinement process continues with every step of the inner growth process. Consequently life has the potential to become clearer and better over time.

Another example would be my own experiences with developing this understanding of refinement. Initially, for too many years, the challenges of life resulted in feelings of disappointment and frustration, again and again. I railed and vented frequently at the difficulties and seemingly insurmountable problems that arose with consistent monotony. It was only in recent years that realization set in. Disappointments and frustrations had indeed reduced considerably. There was increased calm and gentleness in my life. Somehow, the inner work consistently undertaken was paying dividends. The perceived struggles had become a thing of the past. Despite this I was deeply grateful for all that had transpired because it afforded opportunities for inner growth and personal development. Without the challenges I would have remained stuck in the same place in life, with little or no progress possible for expanded consciousness and increased awareness occurring. When I reflect on the clairvoyant vision of the never ending rock hewn staircase mentioned earlier I finally realized that often a picture does paint a thousand words.

Change Process

This journey that is called life and the gaining of wisdom is never-ending. It continues through many lifetimes and consequently your consciousness as a divine being is continually self-challenging in order to evolve into the very best possible version of yourself. Along the way there may be rest stops, successes and major insights and understanding attained. These are only temporary as there is always further learning and growth still to be achieved. This is one of the reasons that Maslow's Hierarchy of Needs is limiting. It can only provide definition and understanding from a human perspective. It does not ultimately explore and define the possible soul growth that is potential within every individual. Maybe it was never intended to do that.

Previously I've referred to the junk DNA as being critical to the awakening process, as it activates that higher knowing you have within. If I were to equate the fifth need, self-actualization, in Maslow's hierarchy I'd suggest it would be a decent resonance match with an individual whose junk DNA was in the process of activation. It would not necessarily be fully activated on every level. In other words, such an individual would have an elevated energy frequency in order to be fully self-aware. In one of the public channelling sessions I undertook, the energy of the soul that had embodied as Edgar Cayce explained simply and clearly the evolutionary changes occurring right now. I am including part of that channelling as it's relevant to the concept of self-actualization and it may assist in providing deeper understanding.

Your DNA is expanding and all those junk pieces of DNA are being lit up. The phrase 'lit up' refers to the conscious and unconscious activation that you are creating as you experience life. Through endeavours to become more mindful and holding intentions to living a meaningful life you are actually igniting those junk pieces of DNA. As this occurs there are magnificent and significant changes occurring within. You are actually activating the memory held within of all that you have ever been through countless lifetimes. Along with this, a shift occurs in awareness, ultimately leading to greater multi-dimensional functioning.

This is a significant shift in evolution. Never before has this been done. It has not previously been possible for this to occur at such a rapid rate. It is undeniable that there have been a few individuals who have achieved such mastery. They have achieved it through diligence, intense study and also through focusing solely upon that activation as their significant life mission, or purpose...

Imagine those two strands of DNA happily intertwining and performing their everyday functions within your body. Then slowly one by one by one all those junk pieces of DNA begin to light up, much like a Christmas tree filled with light. However, in your case it is not all at once, it is one piece at a time.

Exactly what causes this to occur? There are a number of factors supporting this change, and not all of them come from changes within the individual. This process has been predetermined. In the process of having it predetermined there has been much work undertaken by those from the invisible realms. The acceleration and intensification of this work have taken place in the last twenty to twenty-five years of linear time. This is only a relatively short time span within a larger historical context.....

There are some consequences or outcomes from this activation. As each of these pieces of DNA is activated you become more aware of aspects of yourself that were not previously known or understood. As a result of this activation it will be easier to have greater understanding of who you really are. In your dreams, for example, you may begin to have recall or awareness of situations that do not exist in the current lifetime. or you may have experiences with such things as déjà vu – the knowing of having been in a place beforehand, even though you have not been there before. You may even have vivid flashbacks to other potential experiences, which are very often dismissed as being due to an overly active imagination.

There are also physiological changes that may occur with the activation. However I stress that activation of junk DNA is a process and is only possible providing you have undertaken serious inner work. This does not mean all trauma pain from all lifetimes needs to be cleared and healed prior to the activation occurring. The activation occurs incrementally with your intent, based upon your actions and behaviors in general. As the activation proceeds it may also result in further pain and discomfort, which are indications that inner change is occurring. The following is an explanation of the physical changes that may occur during this process.

A Christmas tree lit up is a transient thing. A human being lit up is a permanent creation. Those who have preceded and have attained the status of mastery and enlightenment have shown it can be done. You too can become enlightened – filled with light. As you become filled with light the physiology of your body also undergoes changes.

One of the most profound changes of all is that of a reversal, or slowing down, of the ageing process. I am sure that concept holds great appeal. In society there is an expectation that as you reach a certain age you will begin to lose your faculties. Your thinking processes diminish, your ability to be physically agile reduces and then there are all the attendant health issues that result, and are attributed to old age. That is not a natural state. There are civilizations and tribal groups who have attained longevity as a natural state. It is possible for all human beings to live a long, productive life, much longer than is currently acceptable.

The process of activating DNA strands results in a shift, or change, in the cellular structure. As the cellular structure changes all the physiological functions also change.... Also, as you work towards having all DNA strands fully activated and functioning your awareness of reality will undergo a transformative shift. You will be living fully in the moment and will easily be able to move yourself from one location to another. You will come to see this current linear lifetime you have experienced as being somewhat barbaric and toxic. ....

Right now humanity is undergoing this transformation process. In the process there is pain, discomfort, unease and doubt. However, in undergoing this significant paradigm shift there are many attendant benefits. As you progress through this shift both your thinking and emotions will change. Allow them to change. Let go of fear and restrictions. Let go of any limiting beliefs… if you have that consciousness and awareness (of accepting the changes) you will find it easier to undergo this paradigm shift. Individuals who do it consciously will find it easier than those who still hold resistance.

About fifteen years ago I experienced a disturbing and uncomfortable episode of vertigo that lasted several days. Prior to this I had never had vertigo, and had no medical history that may have indicated a problem in this regard. The vertigo was severe and was distressing, to say the least. Mentally I asked the usual questions.

"Is this physical?"
"No" was the clear response in my head.
"Is it energetic?" was my next question.
"Yes"
"Do I need to seek medical assistance?"
"No"
I followed this with, "Why is this happening?"

That particular question was met with silence which continued for the best part of the remainder of the day. The following morning I got up and headed out for my usual morning power walk, albeit somewhat hindered by the lingering vertigo symptoms. In a fraction of a second, what I refer to as a nanosecond, a slew of information flooded into awareness. I heard the words "thinning of blood" and immediately understood that all the years of undertaking serious inner work was resulting in change in my physical body.

Often when undertaking inner work it's assumed that this impacts only the outer layers of the energy hologram. It impacts the outer layers first and over time goes deeper until a point is reached where real physical changes are possible, on all levels. The "thinning of blood" indicated a change in cardiovascular functioning in my body. One of the joys of getting older in years is that it's normal for blood viscosity to change, for blood to thicken. This is the reason the medical profession often recommend that senior citizens take half an aspirin daily, as the aspirin thins blood thereby reducing the likelihood of blood clots and embolisms.

My awareness was that obviously the blood thinning was beneficial, as it surely would be healthier overall. It could possibly enhance longevity and also general health and wellbeing. However, how could it be proved that blood thinning had actually occurred? It wasn't long before several minor incidents demonstrated clearly that my blood had thinned. A small paper cut and the blood flowed. Some dental work and again the blood flowed more than would have been normal for a person of my senior years. It's been that way now since that initial vertigo experience. In fact, there have been other vertigo episodes, with each one indicating another major frequency shift in my energy hologram. Each time there's been improved health, in terms of wellbeing and mental acuity.

While this information is not intended to be a sharing of my health situation it's being described as a way of explaining that energy frequency shifts are subtle and do impact the physical body. Most likely they impact individuals differently. Yet they are discernible on some level. Since the initial vertigo episode I've encountered numerous clients and friends who have also experienced unexpected vertigo, and who like me initially have been flummoxed as to its cause.

Your biochemistry is unique to you. This means that when you experience an energy shift the benefits are uniquely yours. Each person responds differently to the frequency shifts. Still, from all that I've heard from friends, colleagues and clients alike the physical health benefits are felt on some level.

Ultimately, whether you subscribe to Maslow's Hierarchy of Needs or any other model of life and wellbeing, the responsibility for creating and manifesting your life is yours alone. Theories provide insight and hopefully some understanding of the human psyche. The rest is up to you. How curious are you to know more about who you really are? What motivates you to keep exploring and learning? What are you willing to let go of in order to shift your perspectives?

Chapter 12

It began innocuously, a simple regular meditation that promised to be the same as most other meditations. However, there was one difference that I became aware of – a heaviness around my jaw. It was not in my physical body, yet as I sat in a quiet meditative state my awareness noticed the heaviness, the solidness of my jaw. I had no understanding of what it portended or meant.

The meditation continued and suddenly I saw something that surprised me. I indicated (via mind) that I would like to see it again, in order that I gain understanding – if necessary. The image resurfaced. I saw what looked like a hollow pipe (from the inside). Inside the pipe was a round solid object, like a marble but smaller and definitely solid. Just above the round object there was another line/trajectory that was almost perpendicular to the inside of the pipe that was situated in a north-south direction. As I glimpsed this schematic my awareness recognized this was the inside of my heart. The round shape (marble) was old, dense emotion that needed to be released.

As soon as this knowing emerged I began work. Immediately I knew that this solid round object could not be pulled out directly as it would result in considerable stress on the physical heart. Instead, using both mind and energy I brought in golden thread which was then wound around and around the solid shape, and this was then carefully lifted slightly away from the perpendicular trajectory. It seemed as though this solid shape was then suspended in a space that was less confined or constricted. Next I brought pink light, the energy of unconditional love, to the suspended shape and bombarded it with the healing light. It was a slow and steady process and its disintegration meant that it was able to disperse and release naturally via the blood system.

After that I was guided to visually check the remainder of my heart. The round solid shape had been situated at the back of the right side of the heart.

I found some plaque located in the artery in the left ventricle area. Next thing my mind and energy created something that looked like a bottle brush, which was brought in and scoured away the deposited plaque. Once that was completed the rest of my heart was given a visual scan to ensure that everything was clear. It was!

No sooner had this occurred than I felt warm tingling sensations going through my etheric bodies. I saw something being placed over my heart center, and immediately recognized it as a new energetic heart. Its distinct strong pale blue color was evident. I saw it being placed directly over the center of my heart. There was a momentary period of adjustment as it was settled into position. Shortly after, I began to feel energy moving from this new heart center to different parts of my body. Energy radiated outwardly in all directions. As this was happening my awareness alerted me to the fact that my cells were being activated to this new energy. The sensation was extremely relaxing and it was not long after this that I emerged from my meditation feeling refreshed and relaxed. The meditation had taken no more than half an hour, though it had seemed timeless. (Journal, 2007)

After that particular meditation, visualization and energetic clearing my physical body experienced a reaction, which lasted the whole day. I was intensely cold and shivered constantly. By the end of the day I was in bed early with lights out by nine o'clock. Sleep that night was deep and lasted eleven hours. The following day I felt extremely lazy. My body felt floppy relaxed. I felt weightless and without energy. Time was needed to allow for the integration of the energy work into the physical functioning of my body.

I'm sharing this particular journal entry as it describes an experience I had of using mind and intention constructively. On a conscious level it was not my plan to undertake the delicate clearing out of my energetic heart. I had no inkling of there possibly being an issue. It was my higher wisdom that knew exactly what was required. If that clearing had not occurred most likely at some stage in my life I would have experienced a heart attack or some other physical heart related condition. My body's reaction over the next forty-eight hours was also interesting to observe. It indicated strongly the relationship that exists between the energetic and physical levels within the energy hologram. The connection and correlation between functioning of the physical and energy aspects cannot be ignored or denied.

Relying completely on thought and mind for your existence, and using those as the sole basis for gauging your health and wellbeing is both ineffective and inaccurate. The non-physical component of your being is the core that supports every aspect of your life. Relying on memory and education to provide answers and solutions to life challenges is both short-sighted and limited.

When you depend fully on your intellect and on previous experiences to support you through life and its countless trials you are depriving yourself of the potential to tap into your higher wisdom, your soul knowing. You may from time to time listen to your intuition. Most likely you'll find that when you do listen to your intuition, or inner voice, that things have a way of working out ideally. When you ignore that inner knowing that's when outcomes aren't generally satisfactory.

Albert Einstein is reported to have said, "I think ninety-nine times and I find nothing. I stop thinking; swim in silence, and the truth comes to me". How is it possible to develop and strengthen that inner knowing? Why is it important? What does it offer, in terms of supporting you constructively when decisions and choices need to be made? Only you can figure out the answers to these questions as your experiences and inner knowing are special and apply solely to you.

Based on my experiences there are three ways of accessing, connecting with and establishing an ongoing link to your non-physical consciousness and wisdom. Here I mean having mindful intent in setting up a strong line of communication, in order to further learn and understand yourself and the meaning of life better. There are other ways, often subtle, such as meditation, understanding animal symbolism and so on. Instead, I'm sharing what have been the predominant means by which I've been able to access higher wisdom, which has furthered my learning. The three ways I share may help you explore unfamiliar possibilities. Ultimately it's important that you work with whatever feels appropriate to your particular situation.

Connecting with Non-Physical Beings

As shared throughout this narrative I've mentioned my non-physical companions as being wise, gentle and supportive. I've always seen them as being of non-human form, in other words as extra-terrestrial multi-dimensional entities. Their energy form, often hazy, has consistently been of shapes that are not evident upon this planet. In addition to seeing them clairvoyantly I also became adept at recognizing their energy signature, or vibration. Their presence was felt as a warmish vibration that increased in intensity as it neared my body, often along the right side. Additionally, I would hear a voice speaking inside my head. The words used and syntax were generally at odds with my own particular speech pattern. Sometimes the language structure sounded old fashioned. Nevertheless the information provided has consistently been unerringly encouraging and correct. Their wise tuition has supported learning and understanding to a depth and level that I doubt I'd have experienced in a tertiary institution.

Gradually I came to view the non-physical beings as a form of intelligent energy consciousness. The consciousness I connect with holds varying levels of frequency, most often being of a high level. My way of connecting with these beings is via the energy matrix web that weaves throughout all of creation. It's as simple as placing an international phone call. While I make it sound easy I can guarantee that the learning process has been far from straightforward, easy or comfortable. At times it's been extremely uncomfortable and perplexing.

My personal odyssey has been to shift my level of frequency to a sufficiently high level in order to maximize my learning. That is my part of my life purpose or intention. It's not the same for everyone. Over a period of years that communication and connection has changed. I no longer hear the voice in my head. Instead, I simply know and that knowing flows throughout my body in relation to how best to function and enjoy life. I know what I need to know and do. As absurd as that sounds it actually is an easy way to live as there is no longer any time wasted on attempting to figure out possible options or decisions that need to be made. Initially I relied on their wisdom to provide guidance, and answers to issues wherever possible. Ironically I was never given straight answers or solutions. Instead, often I was provided with cryptic messages or some possibilities – never direct answers or clarification!

Nowadays I know when they're around. I feel their energy signature, or vibration, as it gets close. Their presence is outside of my energy hologram, not within. At times they undertake psychic surgery, which entails upgrading or downloading new energy frequencies. That's all part of the refinement process mentioned in the previous chapter. Infrequently I ask for healing and correction of health issues that may be present. Occasionally I simply request an energy healing session because on some deep level I feel that it's needed. Other times there's a download of information from them. This may relate to matters pertaining to Mother Earth, humanity or potential issues or events. On occasion I may even channel a message to friends or clients. My non-physical friends do not interfere with human decisions or attempt to sway me in any way. Expressed very baldly, they are a great support team yet at all times I'm in the driver's seat regarding the direction and choices to be made in life.

It is not my intention to describe or explain how to connect with non-physical beings, often described as guardian angels, ascended masters and so on. There is ample spiritual literature available that explains steps involved, possible pitfalls, and which includes greater in-depth explanations. However, if you already have a decent connection with non-physical beings you'll know its value in enriching the quality of your life.

Higher Self

In addition to connecting with non-physical intelligent consciousness for guidance I strongly advocate becoming best buddies with your higher self. For ease of understanding and consistency I'm using the term "higher self" to describe that ineffable, non-physical part of you. This is the eternal component that holds memory, has extensive higher wisdom and encompasses the essence of who you are in physical form. Theologians discuss at length the nature of soul, spirit and other aspects of the etheric dimensions. For ease of explanation I use the term "higher self", as a way of referencing that magical, all-knowing and eternal consciousness that exists by you. It does not necessarily reside within you, which was part of my learning in the early days of embracing what I'd now loosely refer to as spirituality.

Early on I'd heard the words "higher self" and learned what it was about without actually understanding what it truly meant. It was not until I was deep in meditation more than twenty years ago that the concept began to intrigue me. In one particular meditation I psychically saw a gold being some distance from me. Mentally I asked, "Who are you?"

The response was immediate, "I am you, your higher wisdom".

The dialogue continued for a brief while, as I was curious to know more about this unexpected encounter. Eventually I asked, "Why are you there? If you're me why aren't you right here, where I am?"

The response wasn't as expected. "You are not ready."

"Will I ever be?"

"Yes. Your body isn't ready."

That reply left me somewhat puzzled. At that stage I was still reading mystical books, which provided some insight as to what was happening. Spiritually aware friends were also asked, and the topic became my favorite subject of discussion for a while. Eventually I learned that my individual frequency needed to be raised before merging could occur. At the same time I engaged in discussion with higher self at every opportunity. I learned that higher self uses words sparsely. There were no long explanations or conversations. Often a simple "Yes" or "No" would be provided when complex questions were asked. Every now and then I'd ask if higher self was ready to meld or merge within me. For a long time the same answer would be given – "It is not time".

In the meantime, however, I noticed that this aspect of myself slowly came nearer and nearer. Anticipation sat strongly within. This was going to be momentous when it happened. Realistically I had no idea at all as to what could be expected. I simply felt it was important to my personal inner growth. Eventually my patience was rewarded. The conversations had become deeper. I asked questions about my purpose, about emotional wounds, relationships and also about the world at large. There was no shortage of questions pouring out of me. Answers were always brief and succinct. It felt as though I had a personal and private tutor explaining life in new ways and with deeper meaning, especially as it related to my personal life journey.

When the merging occurred I was deep in meditation. I sensed and saw an energy mass to my right. It inched closer. Very slowly and gradually it moved into my body (energy hologram). It felt warm and was most definitely buzzing. I sat with the sensations and expressed deep gratitude. The buzz lasted for quite a while. And the conversations continued as previously.

Over time I understood that higher self is the fount of all the knowledge and wisdom I'll ever need. It is able to connect with and access the universal and galactic consciousness. It is plugged in to all of creation. Its wisdom is infinite. It is an aspect of All That Is. It is the source that I connect with when seeking confirmation or information. Higher self is fully integrated and can be likened to being connected online, where the database storage is vast and unlimited.

It is easy to look elsewhere, outside of yourself, for answers and guidance. No one else is you. No one else has the same purpose or history. You are truly unique and special. This is why I advocate connecting with your higher wisdom, your higher self because all the answers you seek are already within you, within your broader scope. You have the capacity to access this on a regular and permanent basis. This magical energy matrix that weaves through the cosmos is part of you, just as you are part of it. There is absolutely no separation.

Earlier in my narrative I mentioned the "voice of the soul". I briefly stressed its importance without actually going into greater detail. In psychological language there are three Ids – conscious, subconscious and super-conscious. I view the super-conscious as being the higher self. It is the ultimate storage facility of all knowledge and as an added bonus has the capacity to access higher wisdom. Conscious mind is ego based, higher self is not. If you are unsure of the actual delineation between ego mind and higher self I highly recommend the book *A New Earth* by Eckhart Tolle. Higher self over rides the ego mind in terms of wisdom and inner knowledge. It provides guidance and insight relating to the true nature of your life and purpose.

As you merge with your higher self you'll find that it becomes increasingly impossible to speak with the voice of ego. Higher self (soul) is the voice of your truth and authenticity. It speaks with love, tolerance and acceptance. You will find that words are expressed of their own volition, powerful words that reflect the real nature of who you are. Ironically, remembering what you've actually said becomes a challenge. This is because the ego mind contains emotions and fears, and loves to judge and create havoc. Higher self expresses itself without attachment. Words of knowing and wisdom flow effortlessly. They have a ring of truth. In an ideal world we would all be speaking from the soul (higher self) and would experience a totally different reality to what is currently occurring. Yet, it is a worthy aspiration because speaking with the voice of the soul truly enables you the potential to manifest a life that reflects innermost truth and desires.

Body's Vibratory Responses

In Chapter Ten I explored the vital role of heart centered intelligence in expanding your consciousness. Body talk is the third way I access the non-physical for guidance and direction. The body talk response originates from your heart center. My body's response to people, situations and issues is a clear indication of whether something is correct or otherwise. The messages the body emits in a vibratory manner are minute, though nevertheless very clear.

Another way of expressing this simplistically is to assert that non-verbal language provides the key to understanding your surroundings, and the people and situations that are occurring. A great deal of analytical and critical information has already been provided on the topic due to social science research into the phenomenon of non-verbal communication.

Your body's responses to people and issues are your initial indicator of whether there's a positive, neutral or negative spin on what is occurring. Figure out what the subtle responses in your body say and you'll soon become even more adept at reading the non-verbal cues. At the very basic level your body will register a positive or a negative response. Not everyone registers a neutral response. For me, a positive response manifests as a warm, fuzzy feeling throughout my body. Other people may feel a light hearted feeling within. It's a matter of personal recognition. I learned that a neutral response entails feeling absolutely no response within. This neutral response is especially helpful when figuring out what health supplements are most suited to my body. A negative response is often a clenching sensation in the lower stomach region.

The more often you respond according to your body's subtle signals, by taking action or otherwise in recognition of the message, the keener and sharper your insights become. As your frequency shifts to higher levels of functioning not only will you understand the subtle messages from your body you'll also be able to extrapolate additional insights or knowing. For example, I find it a common occurrence to know in advance where a person goes with their story lines. At times I know exactly what words will be spoken next. In addition, the underlying emotions also readily become apparent.

Plugging In

It does not matter how tuned in you are, or how little your awareness is in terms of connecting with the non-physical information that's readily available via the cosmic energy matrix. What is more important is your intention and motivation. Are you truly keen to know yourself better? Are you seeking an explanation of your life purpose? Or, are you simply interested in understanding more of what you know exists outside of your current experiences and understanding?

The answers you seek are already there. They exist in this marvellous microscopic web of life that connects everything throughout our known creation. This matrix-like web is the key that unlocks the doors to your exploration and understanding. Earlier I shared a quote from Nikola Tesla, which is worth repeating. It is:

"If you want to find the secrets of the universe, think in terms of energy, frequency and vibration."

Book learning, while invaluable, will only take you so far in your quest. In order to expand your consciousness, a journey of exploration into the world of energy, frequency and vibration offers the opportunity for enhanced expansion and growth. You are entrained within the universe. You participate and contribute to its overall functioning and status with every thought and emotion you hold. This process of consciousness expansion entails more of an experiential growth approach rather than a rigid, regurgitated book learning experience. Ultimately it's about choice – your choice.

The benefits of an energy enriched mindful learning process are plentiful. All areas of your existence – physical, mental, emotional and spiritual – are stimulated and have the potential to enrich daily life in new and exciting ways. Realistically you'd be keen to know there are benefits or positive outcomes to working constructively with energy. It requires commitment, effort and time. The incremental changes and improvements, however, are well worth it.

My experiences are not the only gauge I use to determine the value and worth of understanding and working constructively with energy, frequency and vibration. Mentoring and supporting clients has provided a wealth of confirmation as to its efficacy. Based on my experiences and those shared by others, some benefits and changes are subtle and gradual whereas others are profound. Below I share some of the outcomes or improvements that have come to my attention over the many years I've been privileged to enjoy and work productively with energy.

Physical Body Benefits

The two most significant changes I've noticed are dramatic. Earlier I shared briefly the episodes I've had with unexpected vertigo, which was severe initially. Later episodes were minor and brief in comparison. The actual thinning of the blood that occurred in my fifties was due to the discipline applied consistently. This discipline involved meditation, breath work, undertaking forgiveness, giving gratitude, letting go of attachments and expectations, letting go of programs and beliefs, living in the moment, learning self-love, and more. In other words, a consistent application of self-help practices reached a tipping point within my physiology which resulted in my blood thinning. Thinning of the blood indicates a healthy cardiovascular system, less likelihood of blood clots, embolisms, aneurisms or even the likelihood of heart attack. It also supports the strong functioning of all other body systems and organs. As for the tipping point? I understand it to be that my individual frequency had undergone sufficient shifts – become higher and clearer – for this to occur.

The second obvious improvement has been with yoga. When it comes to doing yoga poses my body's become somewhat of a pretzel. The tension within my body has released to such an extent that yoga poses that once were extremely difficult or downright impossible are now undertaken with greater ease and flexibility.

Over a period of twenty plus years my diet has become even greener and cleaner. When unsure of what to prepare for a meal I often get an image of what my body would like, meaning it would benefit from specific nutrients at that time. Eating a plant based diet that is free of toxic chemical sprays and mostly organic ensures my body is still fit and strong. When I channelled the energy of the soul that embodied as Edgar Cayce he commented that a body holding a high frequency requires nourishment that holds a high frequency. Basically he stressed that processed and refined foods, and those grown with toxic chemicals were damaging to the higher frequency vibration. Clients have also consistently commented they no longer are able to consume meat and other animal products because they taste the emotion of fear in the flesh of the animal that's been slaughtered.

While many seniors often experience hair loss, mine grows in profusion which it never did when I was younger. Another common symptom found in seniors is very thin skin, which bruises easily. Once I became serious about eating organic, clean foods my skin gradually thickened once again. Matching the frequency of the food to the frequency of the physical body naturally brings about healthy life-sustaining functioning.

Other evident benefits experienced include regaining strong senses. My eyesight has changed. I no longer wear glasses, which I'd worn consistently for over twenty years. As my emotional wounds healed my eyesight steadily improved. Hearing remains sharp and acute despite the encroaching years. Sense of smell is also keen, often to my displeasure. Sense of taste has sharpened, with preference only for foods that nourish and heal.

Is it likely the benefits listed, or even some physical body improvements are able to ensure longevity? Of that I have absolutely no idea. Nor can I guarantee that the likelihood of illness is non-existent. What I do know is that quality of life is enhanced and improved when the physical body functions well consistently. I also know that the physical body is capable of regenerating to a state of optimal health, provided the right conditions for that to happen are met. You are responsible for taking care of the unique biochemistry that is your physical body. Remember it is contained within, and is part of your energy hologram. Ensure you take time to learn what it is saying and you'll find that benefits ensue.

Emotional Body Benefits

I liken the healing of the emotional wounds as peeling away the layers. Some individuals have innumerable layers, others have fewer. Delving into this murky and complex issue would require years of study in the field of healing therapies such as psychiatry and psychology. It is not my intention to plunge deeply into those subjects. Instead, I'll focus on some of the emotional benefits you may gain when shifting your frequency to a higher level. I'll endeavour to describe how that will feel. Most likely you're already part of the way so hopefully my sharing will resonate.

Energetically the emotional body sits reasonably close to the physical body. Emotions arise from thought, which arise from subconscious memory experiences. Most likely you are a mix of emotions ranging from extreme low to highly positive. As your frequency shifts, due to undertaking inner work of forgiveness, letting go, living in the moment and so on, your responses to issues also undergo a change.

Often I've heard clients question whether there is something wrong with them because emotionally they no longer react as they've always done. This lack of reaction, or even lack of deep emotional feeling, is an indication of an inner shift taking place.

The triggers that once set off memories of grief, anger, pain and so on will gradually diminish until eventually they will no longer have an impact. The day that there is no longer an emotional response is the day for celebration!

You'll find less interest in living in the past or hanging onto memories of past times. In much the same way you'll no longer be waiting for things to change or improve. Your enjoyment will be with what happens in the current moment. Then once that current moment is over you'll be grateful for the experience without continually re-visiting it.

Other people's opinions and expectations no longer matter. This is a biggie for many people in our culture due to societal conditioning. The subtle pressure to measure up to the societal norms is strong and impacts you emotionally. When you finally let go of responding to that pressure, and become who you really are is the day you've healed emotions relating to self-worth, self-acceptance, self-love and so on. At times when I've inadvertently been emotionally affected by another's comments or viewpoint I mentally remind myself of *The Four Agreements* by Don Miguel Ruiz and quietly affirm, "Take nothing personally". That brief statement is powerful, as it supports an energetic distancing from the emotion, instantly creating a feeling of inner calm.

Your level of attachment and expectation to everything gradually disappears. The Buddhist faith teaches the importance of non-attachment and of having no expectation. Their teachings stress the importance of being present with whatever is happening. As you progress toward this emotional space you'll feel less stressed, anxious or tense. This enables you to fully appreciate whatever is happening right now.

Your level of gratitude and appreciation expands. Simple, small things that once you would have overlooked may fill your heart with joy. You become compassionate and see the beauty in everyone and everything. You understand the hurt and pain in others without judgment.

These are some of the benefits of undertaking deep inner work and letting go of fears, beliefs and subconscious programs. Enjoying a higher level of frequency definitely pays off because of enriched sweetness in life. One change that is especially important is that your inner work impacts your family through the generations. As you change within you'll find, over time that your relationship with family members is also likely to change and often improve greatly. In instances where this does not happen the issue is not you and you'll find it easier to accept the situation rather than attempting to change anyone. The reality is that you can only change yourself, no one else. As a consequence of shifting your inner emotional reality to one consisting of greater harmony you'll find that your outer reality reflects back those changes.

Mental Body Benefits

Already I've shared extensively the importance of using thought/words wisely and constructively. As you progress along this journey of exploration of your language usage and its impact you'll find that benefits will often come slowly. This is because the process involves reprogramming your subconscious memory. In some instances it's taken me three to six months to begin noticing changes, as they were subtle despite being significant. The benefits have included feeling happier within, a constant improvement in language used and also increased manifestation abilities.

In one instance I worked with a client who'd experienced horrific, ongoing abuse for years and whose self-esteem was low. She was motivated to change her life and to leave behind the memories of years of mental and emotional suffering. Intuitively I sensed that she was sensitive and that change could possibly take time. In addition to offering energy healing sessions I suggested that she keep a gratitude journal. Her instructions were to write in the journal daily. I stressed the importance of dating each entry and listing at least one thing for which she truly felt grateful. After a month of undertaking this simple, yet powerful exercise she was a transformed lady. Her mindset had shifted completely, she was optimistic about life and her ability to shift beyond the pain and misery she'd endured. Her language had changed greatly. She was relaxed and able to laugh. The transformation was substantial, and far exceeded any hopes I may have had. The magic ingredient that she possessed within was an inner determination to change her life.

Less mind chatter is another real benefit. Taken further you may find that you will experience moments of blissful non-thought. Once you experience this state you will find your ability to do this continues to strengthen. Whether you choose meditation, breath work, martial arts or a combination of these is irrelevant. Whatever feels appropriate to your needs can produce remarkable results, in terms of energy frequency shifts. This is because your real inner knowing, via higher self, is able to express its needs and to guide you to fulfilling your life purpose.

Spiritual Benefits

Spiritually this is a journey of inner growth. There is actually no beginning and no end. It is basically a journey, with you in the driver's seat and without directions to guide you. Benefits and learning gained along the way are yours to savour. They may include minor shifts in understanding the nature of reality. Or, you may experience moments of bliss and ecstasy, where you feel complete oneness with All That Is. In between there may be instances of deep, intense appreciation of something as straightforward as the scent of a rose or the love bestowed by an animal companion.

Energetically I have eschewed the shackles of religious teachings as well as the beliefs often inherent in spiritual teachings. Instead I have found my own compass directions back to the essence of who I am really. My origins are not from here. Wisdom held within is from elsewhere, yet is also applicable universally. There are no constraints to the ongoing learning that occurs with every minor and major shift in frequency and consciousness.

Over a period of three years I was fortunate to channel the energy of the soul that embodied as Edgar Cayce to audiences in the States. During this time there were questions asked by individuals about health, career, life purpose and other core issues. In one instance there was a question relating to an incident and the individual asked what the lesson was pertaining to that particular incident. The response during the channelling was emphatic. It was:

> "Why does there have to be a lesson? It is because of the teachings of the churches…. Unfortunately, from where I sit now I'm able to see a bigger picture. I see control and power by those who lay down the law as to how things are. When it comes to lessons, that's not what life is about. Lessons are a man-made concept."

During this particular channelling it was stressed that life is about having experiences and that you learn, develop understanding and grow from having a variety of these. This, to my perspective, is a kinder and gentler way of viewing the meaning of life. It is all inclusive of everything and non-judgmental of anything. When viewed this way there are energy frequency benefits. You are likely to be less engaged in mental questioning and have reduced emotional angst. This ultimately supports greater acceptance and valuing of self and of the challenging foibles of living within a duality existence.

Understanding yourself, the nature of who you are and your overall purpose involves a complex and often confusing journey. It's an exciting time to be alive. You are undergoing massive energy shifts and are being fully supported on every level. Everything is changing daily. This is because you, as a dynamic, consciously aware being are also changing energetically on every level. It's an evolutionary process. Take it one step at a time. Be open to appreciating and enjoying the possibilities. This is not a time for the faint-hearted. Become fearless and maintain the eternal vibration of unconditional love you hold within strongly at all times.

****

A lengthy poem entitled "As I Began To Love Myself" has been widely attributed to Charlie Chaplin and was believed to have been written when he was age seventy. I have no way of gauging the veracity of this; though I feel it encapsulates the journey back to the authentic self. There is some disagreement about the author of the poem, and some sources claim it was penned by Kim and Alison McMillen who entitled it as "When I loved myself enough". I'm including a verse from it as this may inspire you to undertake an internet search for the rest of the poem, and to reflect on the wisdom it imparts and possibly its relevance to your inner growth into expanded consciousness.

As I began to love myself I recognized that my mind can disturb me and it can make me sick. But As I connected it to my heart, my mind became a valuable ally. Today I call this connection "WISDOM OF THE HEART".

(From: www.raiseyourvibration.com/as-I-came-to-love-myself-poem-by-charlie-chaplin)

References

Books/Articles

Braden, Greg - "The Divine Matrix" (2007)

Brennan, Barbara Ann - "Hands of Light" (1988)

Day, Phillip – "The Mind Game" (2002)

Emoto, Masaru Dr – "The Hidden Messages in Water" (2005)

Fritjof, Capra - "The Tao of Physics" (1999)

Goswami, Amit – "The Self-Aware Universe" (1993)

Grandics, Peter – "The Genesis of Fundamental Forces Acting at a Distance and Some Practical Derivations" (2007)

Hansen, Bente – "Messages From Beyond" (2001)

Hansen, Bente – "Edgar Speaks, Inner Transformation, 2012 and Beyond and Earth Changes" (2011)

Hansen, Bente – "The New World of Self Healing" (2006)

Hawkins, David MD PhD – "Power Vs Force" (2002)

Jaye, Gabriella – "A Square Peg: Conformity Isn't An Option" (2018)

Hay, Louise – "You Can Heal Your Life" (1984)

Hicks, Esther and Jerry - "Ask And It Is Given" (2005)

Krebs, Charles Dr – "A Revolutionary Way of Thinking" (1998)

McTaggart, Lynne – "The Field" (2002)

Newton, Michael – "Life Between Lives" (2004)

Noontil, Anette - 'The Body is the Barometer of the Soul" (2012)

Ruiz, Don Miguel – "The Four Agreements" (1997)

Saraydarian, Torkom – "New Dimensions in Healing" (1992)

Saraydarian, Torkom – "Thought and the Glory of Thinking" (1996)

Sisson, Colin P – "Inner Adventures" (1997)

Talbot, David and Thornbill, Wallace – "Thunderbolts of the Gods" (2005)

Talbot, Michael – "The Holographic Universe" (1991)

Tolle, Eckhart – "A New Earth" (2009)

Weiss, Brian – "Many Lives Many Masters (1994)

Internet Links

http://aihw.gov.au

http://brian.tracy.com/blog/personal-success/understanding-your-subconscious-mind/

http://consciousreminder.com

www.gaia.com

www.happierhuman.com/maslows-hierarchy/

www.simplypsychology.org/maslow.html

www.wikipedia.org

www.huffpost.com/entry/maslow-the-12-characteris_b_7836836

www.2knowmyself.com/subconscious_mind/subconscious_mind_rules_power

www.heartmath.org

www.raiseyourvibration.com/as-I-came-to-love-myself-poem-by-charlie-chaplin

Printed in the United States
By Bookmasters